THE FUNCTIONING OF A BUDDHA'S MIND

THE DIAMOND SUTRA IN DAILY LIFE

THE FUNCTIONING OF
A BUDDHA'S MIND

Prime Dharma Master Kyongsan

Seoul Selection

THE FUNCTIONING OF A BUDDHA'S MIND
The Diamond Sutra in Daily Life

Published by Seoul Selection
105-2 Sagan-dong, Jongno-gu, Seoul, Korea
Phone: 82-2-734-9567, Fax: 82-2-734-9562
Email: publisher@seoulselection.com
www.seoulselection.com

ISBN: 978-89-91913-82-0   03220
Printed in the Republic of Korea

The original Korean edition of this book was first published in 2000
by Dongnampoong.

 Contents

NOTE

1. The "original text" portions in this book were newly translated into English by the translator of this book from the text of *The Diamond Sutra* as recorded in *The Essential Scriptures of the Buddha and Enlightened Masters* in *The Collections of* Won-*Buddhist Scriptures*. The Korean-language text was originally translated from the Chinese by the order of Won-Buddhism.

2. The "interpretation" portions in this book are explanations of the text from *The Diamond Sutra* that are designed to be suited to a modern context, allowing the general public to gain an easier understanding of the Buddha's original intent through interpretations from the author, Venerable Kyongsan.

3. This book used the Revised Romanization system for Korean words appearing in the text. In the case of certain terms and names related to Won-Buddhism, however, it followed the McCune-Reischauer system adopted in the English-language versions of the Won-Buddhism scriptures.

Preface

It seems very impertinent of me to lecture to believers on *The Diamond Sutra*, a key text by Śākyamuni Buddha, and to organize those lectures into a book. I have always considered the process of publishing a book to be one of praying for the incomplete to somehow become complete.

As I present this book, I would like to express my most profound gratitude from the bottom of my heart to the new Buddha, the Founding Master Sot'aesan, and to teachers including Master Chŏngsan and Master Taesan. I wandered around as a truly trifling sentient being before entering this teaching and forming an affinity with the truth on the strength of the heartfelt teachings that I received on the Il-Won-Sang. In this way, I came to study the words of the teachers of humankind who achieved great enlightenment in the past: Śākyamuni Buddha, Confucius, Laotze, and Jesus Christ, among others. Out of all of these, it was *The Diamond Sutra*, revered as the guiding buddhist scripture of *Won*-Buddhism, that

I took as the occasion for my enlightenment, lecturing on it to the followers of the faith, examining it anew, and publishing this book in the spirit of praise for the Buddha.

The Diamond Sutra was originally written down in Sanskrit more than three millennia ago, and subsequently translated into Chinese. There may be some cases where the true intentions of the Buddha became buried in the writing over the course of its translations, and I also suspect that there are areas in which the true meaning has been exaggerated or expressed incorrectly owing to differences in languages.

In approaching this effort, I took as a case for study the question of how I might express the original meaning taught by Śākyamuni Buddha without becoming bound to language and strict usage, and how the Buddha might express his teachings were he to come here today and speak to modern individuals.

In the Sanskrit name of *The Diamond Sutra* (*Vajracchedika-Prajñāpāramitā-Sūtra*), *vajracchedika*, or "diamond," refers to the unbreakable foundation of self-nature inherent in the human mind; *prajñā* to the light of self-nature that ceaselessly surges forth from that foundation; and *pāramitā* to the recovery of the adamantine self-nature and actions based on that self-nature, by using its light to hone wisdom for the practice of a life without delusion. My hope is that you will adopt this essential diamond nature, the *prajñā* light, and the *pāramitā* practice as your standard in studying and practicing *The Diamond Sutra*.

This essential nature, light, and self-nature practice do not exist for me alone. It is a truth that suffuses the myriad phenomena in the universe.

It is a substance that governs the universe; in today's terms, it might be called an "operator" of all things in heaven and earth. Because it is so difficult for us to seek out and understand the principle that exists far outside, we can most easily awaken to and practice this Il-Won-Sang Truth by seeking out the *Diamond Sutra* way in the place closest to us: our own mind.

In human existence, the way in which we use our mind is what ultimately creates happiness and misfortune. Thus, our first task is to find the truth within the mind and to train the mind. Since this is the ultimate task falling upon religion, we, who first find and practice the *Diamond Sutra* way in our mind, will ultimately master the providence that governs the universe.

Finally, I wish to express my appreciation to the lay followers and ordained followers of *Won*-Buddhism who provided the utmost material and spiritual cooperation toward the publication of this book.

With the prayers of Venerable Kyongsan
at the Muhak Sŏn Center in Masan, Korea

THUS DID I HEAR

The Reasons for the Dharma Meeting

Speak!

What exists to make you say, "Thus did I hear"?

It is the great object, concealed within Ananda for eons.

That mind, just as it is, is now right here.

How sad it is, the taint of

the Buddha's giving the name "*Diamond Prajñā*"

All the more graceful is the moonlight brushed by white clouds.

Thus did I hear. One time, the Buddha was staying in Jeta Grove in Sravasti, living with 1,250 great bhikṣus.

When mealtime came, the Buddha put on his cloak, took his rice bowl, and went to the city of Sravasti to beg. As he begged, he visited each home within the city in turn.

Upon finishing his begging, he returned to his dwelling and ate. He put away his clothes and bowl, washed his feet, laid down a mat, and sat down.

Focus on

Ananda, who served Śākyamuni Buddha from a more intimate relationship than anyone else, described the everyday life of the Buddha during the time he was delivering the dharma instruction on *The Diamond Sutra* while staying in Jeta Grove. In this chapter, we will find out about Ananda, learn about the origin of Jeta Grove and the meaning of the Buddha's sequence in begging, and consider the meaning of the Buddha's ordinary, everyday life. I also hope that the reader will meditate over the Sŏn meaning of this chapter.

"Thus Did I Hear"

The Diamond Sutra begins with the words, "Thus did I hear of the dharma instruction on *The Diamond Sutra*." They are spoken by Ananda, the "first of many listeners"—so called because he was said to have served as the closest of the Buddha's ten main students and to have heard the most dharma instructions. As some 1,250 or so students heard this instruction, these opening words can be taken to express the simple meaning of, "If, by chance, someone out there heard differently, I hope he will supplement what I tell you."

Writing implements were not very well developed at the time, and so it was a period in which mental memorization skills were highly developed—listeners paid close attention to a dharma instruction from beginning to end. Today's scripture can be understood as the record of an oral recitation of something committed to memory in this way.

The people who are alive today keep written records. Because of this, it seems as though they lack the ability to listen carefully with the mind, and it has therefore become more difficult for them to apply the Buddha's dharma instruction in their lives and put it into practice.

While it may be difficult to memorize an entire dharma instruction, when we learn deeply within our mind the truly important instructions that must be put into practice and allow them to aid us by summoning them up for practice as we experience and address certain situations, this will be a truly important element in the use of the buddhadharma in our everyday life.

If each of us examines how many dharma instructions we have memorized, committing to memory those instructions by the Buddha that serve as exemplars for our mind, and if, when time permits, we recall those instructions, applying them as topics for discussion with the person next to us in order to solidify our understanding and practice and engrave them deeply upon our mind, I believe we will find ourselves growing ever wiser and shining more brightly in our everyday lives.

I hope that all of you will listen intently to the dharma instructions given by teachers of high dharma, that you will commit them to memory and review the instructions you heard during your moments of leisure in order to understand them precisely, and that you will organize and record those instructions in your own way, reading them to close friends or your children so that the process can serve both as practice for yourself and as edification for others.

Staying in Jeta Grove

The Buddha delivered his dharma instruction on *The Diamond Sutra* mainly while staying in Jeta Grove. I imagine him giving this instruction under the cool shade of a tree to escape the heat, with his students surrounding him. The original name of Jeta Grove was Jetavān-ānāthapinda-dasyārāma, and there is an interesting anecdote behind its construction.

The Buddha, it is said, was walking with his students when he saw a beautiful garden in the forest and declared that it would be nice to build a temple there. At that time, there was a man there named Sudatta, who was given the name of "Anāthapiṇḍada," or "the feeder of orphans and the helpless," for his charitable services to lonely and poor people. So as to not let the Buddha's words be forgotten, he resolved to build a glorious temple there. He wanted to visit the owner of the land, and learned that it belonged to a prince named Jeta, the son of the King of Sravasti. He met Prince Jeta and said that he wanted to build the Buddha's grove. He implored the prince to sell it, but Jeta had no intention of doing so, and said that he would only sell it if it were covered with gold coins. Sudatta, a man of great buddha spirit, immediately set about loading heaps of gold coins into a cart and covering the garden with them. He went back to the prince and asked again to purchase the land. Moved by his buddha spirit, Prince Jeta agreed, and said that he himself would donate a tree to stand on that land. Thus it was, the story goes, that the grove came into being, called the Jetavān-ānāthapinda-dasyārāma to capture the sense of its being Anāthapindada's land and containing Prince Jeta's tree.

As this was an early Buddhist order, one can sense in this story an expedient means of encouraging contributors to participate in the Buddha's works by eternally recognizing the will of Prince Jeta and the charitable spirit of Sudatta.

Where do you spend your money? The behavior of the ordinary human is to spend money on himself and his family alone. Spending your valuable wealth in a worthy place will be an act that makes the world a warm place and elevates your character.

The Buddha's Daily Life

Originally from Sanskrit, the word *buddha* was translated into Chinese as *fotuo* and into Korean, phonetically, as *bucheo*, accompanied by the honorific ending *nim*. We can understand this word to mean "a sage who awakened to the truth of the universe and life and practiced it with his own being." It can also be understood to mean that whoever awakens to and practices this truth is a buddha. The word *bucheo* is also used to refer to that cosmic and immanent entity that we commonly refer to as the "truth" or the "Way."

"Buddha," here, refers to an actual figure from history. He was born the prince of a small kingdom in India around 2,500 years ago. Curious about life, aging, sickness, and death, he abandoned the throne to live eternal life. He fled beyond the walls of the palace and practiced asceticism for a long period of time before finally awakening to the truth of the universe and life. He would go on to put this into practice and propagate the beliefs of Buddhism, delivering infinite sentient beings and achieving the most ideal of characters.

Sot'aesan, the Founding Master of *Won*-Buddhism, called Śākyamuni Buddha the "sage of all sages" and described him as the most outstanding of all the sages who have ever appeared in human history. The daily life of a great sage like the Buddha is a very ordinary one, and the sight of him begging like his students was so ordinary as to seem strange. It makes him feel all too human, all too close to us sentient beings. Yet we have very much deified the Buddha, shaping him into something beyond human character. In the process, we have become further removed from the Buddha— indeed, we have even come to find it difficult to believe that we could be like him.

As the words in Chapter One of *The Diamond Sutra* tell us, we should approach the Buddha in his human aspect, as an ordinary sage who exists on the same plane as we do. We must be wary, however, of the argument that if the Buddha begged in his day, all religious leaders after him should do so. This is a problematic notion. When we consider how the Buddha might act were he here in the world today, it is easy to imagine that he would not beg. He would surely be ordinary, equal, and benevolent, but I am certain that he would find a way of acting that is suited to the world today.

INTERPRETATION

When meal time came, the Buddha put on his clothes, took his bowl, and went to the city of Sravasti to beg. As he begged, he visited each home in turn, poor and rich alike.

Upon finishing his begging, he returned to his dwelling and ate. He put away his own clothes and bowl, washed his feet, laid down a mat, and sat.

The Meaning of the Buddha's Begging

Why did the Buddha personally beg for his food? Why did he have his followers beg? We will examine these questions in this chapter. Before the Buddha created Buddhism, there existed in India a religion called Brahmanism (Hinduism). According to customs passed down from Brahmanism, practitioners would beg for alms, and it appears that the Buddha adopted this custom.

Let us consider the different meanings of the act of begging.

When you beg, you visit different houses and meet many different people with whom you form affinities. Moreover, there is the meaning of edification, as one may come to share the Buddha's dharma instructions, and there is also the meaning of its being an important means of practicing with humility and modesty.

One major obstacle in cultivating the Way is desire. And when we overcome desire, there is another demon awaiting us, namely conceit. Begging was likely to have been a very important means of overcoming this sort of conceit.

As a religion grows and its clerics enjoy special treatment from their followers and from society, they unwittingly come to think of themselves as pure, noble, and wise. As a result, they drift further and further away from humility. Indeed, they become prone to developing arrogant characters. This is not only the case with clerics: lay believers, over the course of a long life of faith, are given corresponding treatment and titles in the community of faith. At such times, the arrogant mind that follows them around like a shadow may take root within their hearts, such that they may find themselves the objects of censure from society.

It may be said that all clerics and believers, if they are to understand the meaning of begging, need to meditate deeply over the significance of the fact that even a great sage like the Buddha engaged in it, putting the empty mind and humility of begging for his food into practice.

Visiting Each House in Turn to Ask for Food

As he begged for food, the Buddha stopped at seven houses, visiting each in turn, rich and poor alike. It is said that his student Mahākāśyapa, who is described as having been the greatest practitioner of the Way among his disciples, always chose only the poor homes when begging, while Ananda always chose the rich homes.

Hearing of this, the Buddha summoned the two students and asked them why they did so. Mahākāśyapa said that the poor were poor today because they did not create blessings in their previous lives, and that through his own begging he was providing a charitable service and an opportunity for them to create blessings. Ananda said that he begged from rich homes because the poor did not have anything to eat themselves, and that if he took their food they would likely be left even hungrier.

The Buddha said that both of them had given good reasons, but he taught them that an even more truthful, equitable, and moderate way would be for them to beg from every house in turn, without distinguishing between poor and rich. We are at all times living under the control of the selfish mind, the inequitable mind, the extreme mind, all of which ask what is more beneficial for us.

We must understand that the noblest actions are those that are equitable and moderate, and live accordingly.

There should always be a sequence to the things we do. Only by observing the proper sequence well do we become successful workers. Practice of the buddhadharma encourages us to succeed in our affairs. In other words, we should live well with an all-embracing will. If we merely believe in the buddhadharma and do not try to do our work well, we cannot be said to have properly understood the buddhadharma. And if we are to work well, we must understand the essence of work and its goals, consider beforehand the practice in the sequence of its pursuit, and execute it methodically. We live in the midst of work. We must always consider its sequence and understand how to do it properly.

> Spring, summer, autumn, winter, each with a different face.
> Betraying its intention with winds, clouds, rain, dew, frost, and snow.
> There is no hidden secret besides this.
> And so we put on our clothes,
> we eat our meals, at times we talk and laugh,
> And the news of "the diamond" has revealed itself here
> in all its detail. Reader, reader, oh ho!

CHAPTER II

TWO FUNDAMENTAL QUESTIONS OF MIND-PRACTICE

Subhuti's Dharma Request

The laughing eyes shared by the gifted *pansori* performers.

The marvelous melodies float their way down as auspcious snow.

No need to chant the beautiful lyrics.

Do we not all inherently hold the answers?

At that time, the Venerable Subhuti arose from the audience, pulled his cloak from his right shoulder and slung it across his chest, placed his right knee against the ground, and spoke, bringing his hands together in respectful prayer.

"O rare World Honored One! The Tathāgata cares most sincerely for all bodhisattvas most sincerely and teaches them earnestly.

O World Honored One! Where should the virtuous male or female practitioner abide with his or her minds after setting the aspiration of achieving Anuttara-Samyak-Sambodhi (unsurpassed, perfectly enlightened right awareness), and how should they subdue such minds?"

Answered the Buddha, "Good, good, Subhuti. As you say, the Tathāgata seeks to care for and teach bodhisattvas well. I shall speak for all of you, so listen well. This is the way in which virtuous male and female practitioners who have set the aspiration of achieving the Anuttara-Samyak-Sambodhi mind should abide with their mind and subdue such minds."

"Yes, World Honored One! We will gladly listen."

Focus on

Subhuti harbors questions about the most basic attitude of mind-practice and the way to subdue mistaken minds. In this passage, he asks the Buddha for a dharma instruction on these questions. With this chapter, we will learn about Subhuti, a distinguished student of the Buddha, and about how the Buddha instructed and led his students. We will also ponder deeply the question of why all humans should become buddhas. I also hope that we will understand about the two fundamental questions for people who hope to attain a buddha's character.

The Buddha's Love for His Students

Of all the Buddha's students, Subhuti was said to understand best the truth of the void, possessing such discernment regarding the principles of the void that he earned the name of "Subhuti, First in Understanding the Void." His name was rendered in Korean as "Subori." His name has also been translated as "Seonhyeon" ("manifesting virtue") and "Seon-gil" ("virtuous and auspicious"). He was said to be one of the Buddha's older students, and was therefore referred to as "Gusu" ("possessing years"). The name "Subhuti" communicates the sense of respect in the Buddhist faith for someone possessed of age, learning, and virtue.

Because the primary principle in *The Diamond Sutra* is the truth of the void, and the Buddha's teaching focuses on how to use that truth, it appears that he delivered his dharma instruction in the form of answers to questions by Subhuti, who among all the audience members had the deepest understanding of this truth.

As the ideal figure in human history, the Buddha was a person of great freedom, liberated from all worldly things. He was the wisest and most merciful of people, and for this Subhuti called him the rarest of respected men in this world. Because the Buddha was the noblest person in this world, he was also called "World Honored One," and because he revealed the very essence of the truth that is just as it is, he was called "Tathāgata." "Tathāgata" is a name meaning "one who has embodied the truth," or "one whose character is that of the truth itself."

Subhuti expressed to the Buddha in two ways that the Tathāgata educates bodhisattvas among the students who cannot match the Buddha's abilities but are just below the level of the Buddha allowing them to become ones with buddha character.

The first way is through "caring" or "protection", which for bodhisattvas means to concern oneself with one's mind. It may have been that the Buddha clearly understood within his mind the progress of the bodhisattvas' practice. He would have thought to himself, "This is where such-and-such bodhisattva is strong, and this is where he is weak, so this is what concerns me." He concerned himself with how he might guide the growth of that bodhisattva to a buddha character. There are no words to describe the care and concern that parents experience toward the child they are raising. In the same way, the buddha's mind is one that takes the utmost care in looking after and tending to his students. This is what is meant by "protection."

A buddha possesses truly wondrous power. The president of a country can easily handle the affairs of state, as his words and deeds exercise great power. In the same way, a buddha, being possessed of the truth, has the power to open the path before sentient beings and to extinguish misfortune through his dharma power by protecting those beings and praying for them with his mind. We must understand this and commit ourselves sincerely to becoming practitioners of the Way who enjoy his protection.

The second way is through "teaching" or "entrusting." These words refer to the bodhisattva personally receiving encouragement and admonitions in terms of what he needs to do. A gardener raising a tree examines the shape of the tree, tends to the branches that should grow to be strong, and clips the branches that must be removed, all the while maintaining the tree's balance. In the same way, the Buddha always delivers the appropriate teachings after viewing the mental and bodily carriage of the bodhisattva. It is a special case when a buddha or teacher delivers direct teachings to one of his many students. He needs to closely and attentively watch that person's facial expressions, hand gestures, and words, honoring them in his mind and understanding their meaning precisely. The words of the scriptures may not be precisely suited to our degree of progress, but words spoken directly to us are always the most appropriate teachings for our situation. We must therefore have profound faith so that we enjoy this encouragement. The greatest of all religious teaching is that which is transmitted by the mouth and received by the mind. We must commit ourselves sincerely so that our relationship is that between a student and a transmitting teacher.

Parents raise their children with a great love. The mind of mercy in the buddha as he brings about progression in bodhisattvas is likewise intense. It may be said that while the parents' love for their children has little educational effect because of the fixation involved, the buddha offers the proper teachings after seeing his students correctly, without any sense of attachment, and his teachings thus have a far greater educational effect.

Do you have a teacher you admire and view at all times as a standard for emulation? If so, do you sense his protection, and do you sense the teacher's praise and occasional censure as the mind of mercy? Or do you perceive it with a disappointed or skeptical mind? We must keep in mind that the person engaged in mind-practice will enjoy far swifter progress with his practice if he has a teacher to protect and encourage him, and if he accepts that protection and encouragement without question.

"O World Honored One! What mind standard should the male and female practitioner adopt once they aspire to attain the unsurpassed, great Way, and how should they subdue mistaken minds?"

The Virtuous Man and the Virtuous Woman

Among the people of this world, we see those who have a religion and those who have none. Even within the former group, I believe that there are several stages. First, we have those with a conventional or ceremonial faith in their religion. Next, we find those whose belief is informed by a slightly deeper awakening. In Buddhism, the terms "virtuous man" and "virtuous woman" are used to refer to those who approach the truth of religion with this deeper sense of awakening.

The virtuous man or woman is fervent in his or her practice of faith, with the goal of connecting religious teachings with his or her own life, and thus living a new life.

As the virtuous man and woman continue with their exertion, they necessarily come to aspire to reach the truth. Up to this point, they have merely had a vague sense of belief and followed along with the teachings of the Buddha, or whatever their religion may be. Now, however, they have arrived at the profound resolution to make the religious teachings their own. This is also referred to as "practice." It is a progression from the stage of belief—as when a child believes in and relies upon his parents and simply does as he is told—to a development stage in which the desire emerges to make the truth one's own, as when a child grows older and develops his own autonomy. Of this process, it can be said that one has passed through resolution and entered the stage of practice. Among virtuous men and virtuous women, there are those who are in the stage of belief and those who are in the stage of practice.

The Aspiration to Reach the Truth

"Anuttara" means "the unsurpassed," the person who practices the highest truth. "Samyak" means "right and all-pervasive," describing the truth and the character that are rightly pervasive. "Sambodhi" means "right awareness," referring to the character with right enlightenment, right principles, and right wisdom.

This describes the buddha, one who has achieved perfect awareness that is broad, right, and unsurpassed. It is therefore used to refer to the great character of one who becomes a buddha and delivers sentient beings. In a word, we can say this is someone who has achieved the unsurpassed great path or greatly perfect enlightenment.

In their lives, people attempt to live well. But what is meant by this? Does it mean getting a good job and marrying, raising children well, making money and earning honors? Doing so requires the use of so many minds! We must suffer and strive, we must create so much transgressive karma to keep these things, and we must worry ourselves amid unforeseen disease and misfortune. It is a terrible uncertainty and anxiety, the fear that the possessions we have obtained may all disappear. All the while, death slowly but implacably approaches.

We must think seriously about our existence and reconsider what it means to truly live well. The Buddha was born into a royal family, and his future as a king was assured. But the Buddha saw the images of birth, aging, sickness, and death and wondered if there was not some eternal life in which one avoided this misfortune, aspiring to venture out in search of the Way. So special was this resolution that he abandoned the throne as though it were nothing and went in search of the Way, spending a long time practicing asceticism before awakening to the Way and eventually becoming a buddha. We, too, can produce this special aspiration.

But all of you who believe in the buddhadharma, and even those of you who believe in other religions, must approach the truth of your religion more seriously, generating the conviction, "I, too, need to live the truly good life. I, too, need to live a life that is free from torment."

The truly good life is not about financial comfort, nor is it about raising children or gaining honors. For all of these things might fall apart at any moment, and they come with the suffering of guarding and amassing them. If, like the sages, we live well in accordance with the truth—the buddhadharma taught by *The Diamond Sutra*—money and honors will follow in due course.

The Two Questions of the Seeker of Truth

The person who has resolved to attain the character of the buddha and live the best life, and the person who has firmly resolved to become a seeker of truth, must begin by asking two fundamental questions.

First, there is the question of where our mind will abide. We can understand this as asking what is the attitude we should maintain with our mind, or the standard we should adopt for its use.

The second question concerns the way in which we must subdue the mistaken minds of desire, distress, and idle thoughts that arise ceaselessly in our mind to torment us.

The person who, after finding a job, sets a goal to become a top manager, rather than remaining an ordinary employee, is certain to ask what mind-set he needs to maintain, and how he plans to eliminate the obstacles that lie in his way to the top.

For the seeker of truth who hopes to become a buddha, two basic questions inevitably arise: how must one use the mind to become a buddha, and how is one to eliminate the wicked minds that get in the way of doing so? It may be that Subhuti asked the Buddha about this because he knew it was a topic of much interest for the audience, having experienced the process himself.

We cannot achieve awakening without harboring questions. When the leader of an organization has no critical mind-set, he cannot bring about growth in that organization. The person without cases for questioning can never be wise.

One cannot become a buddha through the mind of faith alone. When, based on this mind of faith, we have the determination to put what we believe into practice, questions necessarily arise in our mind. If we have the mind of faith and the determination to put it into practice, but we do not harbor questions, we must take this to mean that there are flaws in our mind of faith, or our determination to put our faith into practice.

Just as obstacles lie in our path when we have a powerful drive to succeed, so do questions necessarily follow when we have the powerful determination to practice the buddhadharma.

Do you find yourself facing things that do not work out well in your mind-practice? What do you have trouble understanding when studying the scriptures? You should make this clear to yourself, and turn it into the subject of your questioning. In so doing, you will awaken to a profound truth.

We must bear in mind that those who have no questions in their heads will forever depend on the judgments of others and become stone-headed.

INTERPRETATION

Answered the Buddha, "Subhuti, you have asked a very thoughtful question. As you say, the Tathāgata seeks to care for and teach bodhisattvas well. I shall speak for all of you, so listen well. This is the way in which male and female practitioners who aspire to attain the unsurpassed great path should abide with their mind and subdue mistaken minds."

"Yes, World Honored One!

We will happily hear your dharma instruction."

What Mind to Live With and How to Subdue the Mind

Because he knew the concerns of bodhisattvas, the Buddha was, I believe, waiting for these two questions. The entire text of *The Diamond Sutra* consists of a response to Subhuti's two questions: "Where must we abide with our mind?" and "How can we subdue a wicked mind?" Naturally, we must find out the answers to these two questions in all of their aspects. In the first stage of our understanding, the answers may be, "You must have the mind-set that I have explained to you," and "You must subdue mistaken minds according to my teachings." As our practice deepens, however, we must take heed not only of the teachings above but the teachings that existed before them. There needs to be profound reflection on the sentence that reads, "The person who aspires to attain buddhahood should properly work to maintain this mind and subdue bad minds in this way." This may be called a "meditative interpretation."

When asked, "Where is one to abide with the mind?" the Buddha replies, "It should abide like my mind." Let us consider for a moment what kind of mind the Buddha had when he uttered these words. We must understand his mind at that moment. He stated that it was necessary to keep one's mind as his was. There will certainly be some people who immediately understand this state without its needing to be spoken. Those who do not should study the question of what the Buddha's mind was at this moment as a subject for questioning.

When asked, "How should we bring mistaken minds of gnawing desire, distress, and idle thoughts into submission?" the Buddha clearly states that, "They will be brought into surrender if you abide in my mind at this moment." What kind of mind is this that is capable of eliminating such wicked minds?

When we are teaching our child to write, and he asks, "How do I write the letters 'A' and 'B'?", we respond by writing out those characters and telling him, "This is how it is done." In the same way, the Buddha, before offering any explanation in words, instructed us to keep this particular mind and to subdue thoughts with this mind. Those whose mind's eye is open will see and understand.

When we scrutinize people's behavior, we see how they live their lives floating from place to place without settling. We suffer unrest, and so we develop attachments to things. For instance, we live our lives rooted in feelings of greed for money, for our children, for privileges and honors. In the process, we end up suffering when transformations occur in the objects of our affection. We then turn our attachments elsewhere. The existence of the sentient being is one of cycling through destinies in this way, living its life in search of a place to put its attachment, dying and being born again to experience the same thing. Where, then, did the Buddha keep his mind in his daily life? Would he have lived with attachments to objects with their manifold transformations? What kind of mind was this, the place where the Buddha kept his mind twenty-four hours a day? What kind of mind was this "hometown of the mind"?

So what kind of mind do we have, dealing with the distress and idle thoughts that work like a blazing fire to torment us—the eons of those minds are too vast to count? Typically, we call these the "three poisons and five desires," or the "hundred-eight defilements." It may be that the number of different kinds of defilements is too large for us to fathom. We might go several hundred lifetimes without identifying each of these minds and bringing them into submission. We must find the one mind that eliminates all of these different wicked minds in a single stroke. Only then will we have done well with our practice of *The Diamond Sutra*. The Buddha said that we must subdue the billions of demons with that one mind.

In this way, the mind in which we must abide and the mind with which we must subdue are one and the same. The original intent of our study of *The Diamond Sutra* is to find this one mind.

> For the answer to the question is merely an echo.
> Understanding and teaching, too, are merely shadow play.
> When the curtain falls and the play ends,
> The east person will return home to the east,
> And the west person home to the west.

CHAPTER III

NINE MINDS THAT MUST BE REFORMED

The Orthodox Cardinal Doctrines of the Mahāyāna

Deep in the vast ocean, the fish are without limit.
And so these myriad defilements and idle thoughts
wind sinuously through my mind.
I locate a gold-threaded net, a family heirloom,
Give it a toss and see the goldfish flop about.

Said the Buddha to Subhuti, "All bodhisattvas and mahasattvas should subdue minds in this way: 'I shall guide unto nirvana without residue and thus deliver, among all the types of sentient beings in this world:

those that arose from eggs,

those that arose from embryos,

those that arose from moisture,

those that arose from metamorphosis,

those with form and color,

those with neither form nor color,

those with thoughts,

those without thoughts,

and those that are neither with nor without thoughts.'

Though he may deliver boundless, innumerable, and infinite sentient beings in this way, in truth there is no sentient being that has been delivered.

Why is this so?

Subhuti! If the bodhisattva harbors the conception of the self, the conception of the person, the conception of the sentient being, or the conception of long life, then he is not a bodhisattva."

Focus on

The best way for the human to live is through creating the buddha's character. What, then, must we do to subdue the wicked minds, the ones that get in the way of our achieving a buddha character? We must make the great vow of the bodhisattva, a pledge to deliver all living creatures, and we must engage in practice to rid ourselves of our ignorance and greed and the four misleading concepts, the so-called "high-level" defilements. In this chapter, we will learn about the power of aspiration to achieve buddhahood, about the world of our mind, and about the nine wicked sentient being minds that we must abandon and reform. Also, we will learn about the four misleading concepts.

Said the Buddha to Subhuti, "All bodhisattvas, the outstanding bodhisattvas, should subdue mistaken minds in this way. They must make the great vow to guide and deliver unto the limitless buddha's Pure Land all the sentient beings in this world:

   those that arose from eggs (bewildered minds),

   those that arose from embryos (habit-bound minds),

   those that arose from moisture (melancholy minds),

   those that arose from metamorphosis
   (taste-driven minds),

   those with form and color (stubborn minds),

   those without form and color (empty minds),

   those that are thinking (minds that only think and
   do not know how to act),

   those without thoughts (minds that mainly focus on
eliminating thoughts),

   and those that are neither with or without thoughts
(minds caught on the presence and absence of thoughts).

Moreover, they must engage in sincere mind-practice to convert their own nine types of defilements and idle thoughts that represent the sentient beings in their own minds and turn them into tranquil, luminous, and merciful minds."

The Blight of Defilements That Must Be Subdued

Subhuti asks two questions: "Where are they to abide with their minds, these virtuous men and women and bodhisattvas who have achieved a certain state in their practice and set the aspiration of achieving a buddha character?," and "How are we to subdue wicked minds?" In response, the Buddha first presents a method for subduing minds. We may understand this sequence in his explanation to mean that once we have subdued wicked minds, it becomes easy for us to understand naturally where the mind should rest.

In essence, the Buddha begins by explaining specifically what wicked desires, defilements, and idle thoughts exist to forever torment the interior of the sentient being's mind. He does so in terms of nine types of sentient-being minds, describing the worlds of the human mind in stages according to the concentration of defilements, and also illuminating the world of living creatures and the reality of cycling through births, changing lives after death according to the degree of one's defilements. This cyclical process is articulated in terms of nine types of worlds. Indeed, there truly is a never-ending onslaught of distress and idle minds that roils in the minds of sentient beings, surging like the waves of the ocean.

The Embryo-Born Mind

First, there is the mind of those conceived as embryos. Just as we are born into this world attached to the umbilical cord of our mother, so the embryo-born mind is a mind of stubbornness in which we are instilled with tremendously tenacious habits within our mind. This stubbornness serves simultaneously to sustain, defend, and assault us, creating the everyday basis of our existence. Thus we are constantly tormenting ourselves because of this mind, generating conflicts with those around us, while living a torturous existence.

This mind of stubbornness is an eternal obstacle to our transformation to a new form of existence, with its roots in desires that impede our growth. Our original mind is the no-mind, the void. Yet, when sensory conditions arise, it is this mind of stubbornness that manifests itself, and we provoke corresponding emotions of joy and anger, sorrow and happiness. The person for whom this mind of stubbornness dominates may, with one mistake, find himself cycling into the destiny of the embryo-born sentient being once this life has ended.

The Egg-Born Mind

Second, there is the mind of those born from eggs. This is a mind of constant roaming without any stable center. It is a mind that is forever divided and lacking stability, leading in turn to an existence dominated by some unidentifiable sense of malaise. This egg-born mind, the floating mind, leads us to wander amid solitude, loneliness, and torment.

The sentient being for whom this restless mind dominates could easily end up as an egg-born sentient being when cycling into the next life.

The Moisture-Born Mind

Third, there is the moisture-born mind. This refers to an emotional state in which a person seems to dwell in a place where no rays of sunlight shine, his mind forever dismal and shrouded in darkness. Such a person follows a path in life dominated by the mind without brightness, the pessimistic mind, the resentful mind, owing to previous transgressions or karma from previous lives. He lives with the belief that the world is a dark and dismal place, and so the very experience of life is torturous for him.

This person who lives in darkness, always concealing something within the shadows, is prone to devolving into a moisture-born sentient being once he ends this life and begins the next.

The Metamorphosis-Born Mind

Fourth, there is the metamorphosis-born mind. In such cases, the mind is not fixed, but constantly transforms according to the environment. Just as the peacock adorns itself in various colors, just as the chameleon is fickle and lacks an identity of its own, so this is a life in which thoughts and emotions are constantly transforming, never fixed, with a ceaseless intermingling of joy and sadness, pleasure and pain. Thus it is a life in which the mind is always troubled and experiencing endless discord with its surroundings.

All living creatures, including human beings whose lives are dominated by severe emotional changes and fickleness, are prone to devolving to the status of metamorphosis-born sentient beings when cycling through destinies.

We use the term "sentient beings of the world of desire" to refer to the lives of people dominated by the aforementioned four minds. At its root, this world is dominated by physical desires, and we live our lives according to the places where the karmic power from previous lives weighs heavily. In a word, this is a world controlled by desire, and in ontological terms, the world of denizens of hell, beasts, and human beings.

The Mind of the Sentient Being with Form

Fifth, there is the mind of the sentient being with form. This refers to a mind-state of powerful fixation in the absence of awakening to the Way, where a person values some legal principle or heavenly principle in reality, clings tightly to it, and feels compelled to live his life according to this philosophy.

In this world, we find many people who frequently quibble over matters and argue merely in terms of principles. The term "mind of the sentient being with form" refers primarily to the mind of such a person, owing to the fact that while the mind is formless by nature, this kind of person mainly uses certain minds as though they had form. People in this category are constantly arguing about justice and injustice and measuring the world according to their own philosophy and standards. The result is that they are forever experiencing torment. In terms of their practice level, it suffices, as is often thought, to consider them to be among the cultivated.

The Mind of the Sentient Being Without Form

Sixth, there is the mind of the sentient being without form. This mind constitutes a trap and defilement principally encountered by practitioners of the Way who have not awakened with certainty. These practitioners believe that the world ultimately ends in nothing, that it is empty, and that reality is therefore meaningless. They succumb to nihilism and lead the life of the eccentric, repudiating cultural norms in clothing, food, and shelter. People dominated by this category of sentient-being mind are frequently found at the periphery of religious faiths. They are high-minded sentient beings, suffering from a sort of nihilism disease—misunderstanding the words of the Buddha and wrongly interpreting the realm of the void.

These two categories can be classified as "sentient beings of the world of form." Whereas those in the aforementioned world of desire are dominated by desire, we can view this second type as referring to the form of existence in which one's life is dominated by certain forms of ideas. While it could be characterized as being more sophisticated than the world of desires, the torments are the same, and it is enough to understand that this is an equally mistaken way of living.

The Mind of the Sentient Being with Thoughts

Seventh, there is the mind of the sentient being with thoughts. This category consists of those who speak and write of the world of the buddha, the world of sages—in terms of ideas, reasoning, and discrimination—without awakening to the certain realm of no-mind and the realm of the truth. Such a person mistakes this activity for something worthwhile or stubbornly maintains that it is the best approach, and he disregards other ways or indulges in playing with ideas. One cannot proceed toward ultimate bliss through ideas, nor can one attain a buddha's character. This is a category of sentient being that lives according to ideas and imagination, and it should be avoided at all costs.

The Mind of the Sentient Being Without Thoughts

Eighth, there is the mind of the sentient being without thoughts. This refers to a person who has mistakenly interpreted the buddha's mind as a realm in which all thought has ceased, who argues solely for meditative absorption that is free of thought, and who lives his life engaged in faulty cultivation of the Way. Buddhas often counsel that this kind of insistence merely on practice without thought leads the practitioner into inertness. Such practitioners fail to understand the true reality of the void realm, conceiving of the buddha-mind in idealistic terms and insisting upon a realm devoid of thought. Because the mind is alive, such people are tormented when minds arise, and they will sometimes claim that it is realistically impossible for them to attain the character of a buddha due to their own difficulties and failures.

The Mind of the Sentient Being That Is Neither Without nor With Thoughts

Ninth, there is the mind of the sentient being that is neither without nor with thoughts. Teachings about the mind-realm of the buddha frequently separate it into substance and function, foundation and operation, and this term refers to a truly advanced form of sentient being that lives according to vague ideas and standards—failing to achieve perfectly penetrating awakening to that realm and thinking that minds are both present and absent. This person essentially confuses the pie in the sky with a real pie. People who have exerted themselves in cultivating the Way may enter this existence by mistake and come to dwell there comfortably. But because they have failed to awaken surely in some corner of their mind, we could say that they are constantly being pursued by the shadow of lingering defilements.

These three sentient-being worlds are called the "sentient-being minds of the formless world." Sentient beings that have resolved firmly enough to produce forms are called sentient beings of the world of form. This is the existence of living creatures that may have left behind such stubbornness and fixation, but who still linger in a world of faint ideas.

What Is Your Mind Disease?

Sentient beings must be wary of where they are heading as they cycle through destinies to begin their next life—in other words, when this life comes to an end and they die. As a general rule, a life spent dominated by the egg-born mind, roaming without any fixed center and dominated by a mind of instability, will lead to an egg-born mind in the next life. It is very likely that such a person will be born as something that truly does come from an egg, such as a bird.

We must keep in mind the fact that the destinies into which sentient beings cycle depend entirely on what mind dominates this life, and on where it has fixated.

All of us must think deeply today about what sort of mind dominates our lives. Naturally, there will be some degree of mixture among many different sentient-being minds. But we could say that the person whose path is constantly being blocked by powerful desires has a mind in the world of desire: that of embryo, egg, moisture, or metamorphosis birth; the person whose life revolves around principle in every situation is a sentient being from the world of form; and the practitioner of the Way who is unable to escape the shadow of some false notion or misleading idea is a sentient-being of the formless world. If, however, we make a vow to discover our mind disease, eliminate it, and change our mind to a right one, and if we exert ourselves in cultivating the Way, we will turn the sentient-being mind into our servant.

We are able to produce such a variety of minds because the mind is, in reality, perfect and complete, equipped with all things and capable of anything. The mind is truly gifted, and a single mind can transform into any of the nine types of sentient-being minds. If we succeed in disciplining these minds, we can turn them into the nine minds of the buddha, and even the nine powers of the buddha. Just as all manner of objects exist in the world in the ten directions, we, too, possess all manner of minds. When we awaken to the one mind and train our various minds into ones of value, we will become buddhas of myriad capabilities.

Setting the Aspiration of Delivering Sentient Beings

In answer to the question of how to subdue mistaken minds, the Buddha illuminated for us the nine types of mistaken sentient-being minds. Now, the question turns to how to subdue and train those minds so that our mind becomes the buddha mind—that is, how to lead ourselves into ultimate bliss, make ourselves wise, motivate ourselves to create blessings, and train our mind into one that benefits the world.

The Buddha teaches that we must make a great vow to deliver every single living creature in this world without exception. This vow is an excellent means of subduing the mind. In the world we live in, those who have set for themselves the goal of becoming great individuals are skilled at controlling their own actions. But those who lack any particular wish and are not high-minded are prone to behaving any which way.

When the person who has resolved to become a buddha sets the great aspiration of relieving the suffering of all sentient beings, and compares any personal desires or defilements that arise to his greater goal of becoming a buddha who rescues the nine types of sentient beings, he will necessarily subdue wicked minds to great effect.

In Buddhism, the Four Vast Vows are recommended as great pledges for attaining the character of a buddha.

The first is a vow to deliver all the boundless sentient beings of this world. The second is a vow to eliminate the endless defilements and idle thoughts within our own heart. The third is a vow to learn the immeasurable dharma instructions of the Buddha, and the fourth is a vow to achieve all the unsurpassed capabilities of the Buddha.

In summary, these four vows exhort us to cultivate our own character into that of the Buddha and to give service to the boundless numbers of living creatures. We need to set these aspirations and then reinforce them over and over through prayer with an impregnable power of aspiration. Otherwise, they will end up as just another short-lived resolution—our wishes will fall by the wayside, and we will readily abandon our vow after even the slightest adversity. People suffering from defilements should examine whether their earnest wish to be free from them has been properly reinforced.

The Confucian practitioner who possesses the greater goal of making the nation or people prosper will be cautious and work to rid himself of any selfish interests operating in his mind so that he does not embarrass himself before the people. It is natural for him to do so, and for him to be cautious with his body as well, striving so that no defect arises in the future.

The person with great desires can subdue the small desires in his mind. Parents who love their child will naturally see their selfish desire for personal comfort disappear due to their love for their child. Even when they have not studied methods for educating their children, loving parents receive child education unbeknownst to others due to their mind of love for their child.

The person who has established the goal of becoming a buddha—the goal of worrying for and loving sentient beings—must subdue his defilements and idle thoughts quickly if he is to experience fewer of them. Furthermore, he will develop the wisdom and capability to resolve the difficulties of others. If we are lazy about eliminating the defilements and idle thoughts that arise in our mind, we can judge this to mean that our vow to become a buddha has weakened.

If ignorance and defilements arise here and now, we need to reinforce and reflect upon our goal of becoming a buddha. When we do, the idle thoughts will most often disappear.

Return to the Original Mind

We must dissolve the vermin of mind defilements with *nirvana*. Because ignorance and greed cause our minds to burn, and the defilements within gnaw at our minds like blights of germs and insects, we have been driven out of the paradise that we were originally given.

There is a buddha realm of ultimate bliss that all of us carry in our minds—a buddha mind that is tranquil, luminous, and merciful. We call this the "realm of *nirvana* without residue." The meaning of *nirvana* is "extinguishing," likening defilements such as desire to flames that are snuffed out. When we extinguish the defilements and idle thoughts that arise, the realm that remains is one of ultimate bliss, the kingdom of the Buddha.

When a defilement arises in our mind, we must immediately say, "Desire has begun to operate," and rid ourselves of that mind or assess it against the original mind that is free of defilements. It may not go away the first time, but if we frequently make sincere, committed attempts to assess and eliminate such defilements, they will lose strength and be extinguished.

However limitless the manifestations of the nine types of sentient-being minds may be, when we assess them repeatedly and with sincere commitment, the realm of ultimate bliss will be revealed—the original mind that has let go of all suffering and all pleasure.

When a child has just entered elementary school and begun to study writing, he is very unskilled at it. If he continues with his practice, however, he will become a master calligrapher. When we begin mind-practice and perform it consistently for some time, we may be astonished at the number of defilements that we discover and consider abandoning our practice. But if we refrain from abandoning our practice and work instead to dissolve these defilements with the original mind of the self-nature, there will come a day when we subdue that greed and those defilements. This may be called "the practice of reflection on the original mind." When we continue with this reflection on the self-nature, there will arise in us the capability to understand the minds of other sentient beings, as well as the dharma power of unlimited mercy capable of bringing those minds into submission.

The Fundamental Mind without Either Sentient Beings or Buddhas

One of the koans reads: "It is said that the World Honored One descended into his royal family without leaving Tusita Heaven and delivered all sentient beings while still in his mother's womb. What does this mean?" Once, when I was working on administrative duties at Youngsan University of Sŏn Studies in Baeksu Town, I walked over to the town office from the university. On the way, I saw a village and some children playing beneath a tree. I wanted to ask them where the town office was, and without thinking I said, "Child, where is Baeksu Town?"

Naturally, one of the children answered, "*This* is Baeksu Town."

I felt as though I had heard something truly disconcerting—I was looking for Baeksu Town in Baeksu Town.

All defilements and idle thoughts are buddha minds, and sentient beings are all buddhas. This is the reason for the saying "everywhere a buddha image." That is precisely the meaning of this saying. However many sentient beings a buddha may have delivered, he is no different from them in terms of the realm of nature and the realm of principle. In other words, neither the buddha nor the sentient being has left the nature or principle behind entirely.

One day, Suun was visited by a student who asked him, "Where does the Lord of One Heaven Hanullim dwell?"

He answered, "My daughter-in-law is the Lord of Heaven. She's over there by the loom weaving hemp cloth."

The student could not grasp his meaning. We may understand the meaning of this story if we understand this koan. Before those who have delivered sentient beings can eliminate the false notion of their having delivered them, they need to understand without question this realm in which no distinction can be made between the sentient being and the buddha.

If, in the midst of suffering from defilements and idle thoughts, we consider whence our suffering came, we will see that it emerged from our own realm of self-nature.

The name "weed" has been attached to certain plants because they are not needed by us humans—even though they make an outstanding foodstuff for sheep and other animals. Likewise, our various minds become problems for us because they are not suited to a particular time and place, but all of them are needed. We need love for our children so that we can raise our children. The problem arises when we fixate on this. Thus, in the final analysis a defilement is a mind that is not suited to a certain time and place, and the mind of enlightenment is one that is suited to the time and place.

Just as the use of a house changes with its owner, so all of our defilements and idle thoughts will transform into the buddha's mercy when the owner of our mind becomes a buddha, and so our body will become a slave to desire if desire becomes its owner. When the buddha mind becomes the owner, our body becomes the body of a buddha.

"Why is this so? Subhuti! If the bodhisattva has the idea that he is noble [the notion of self], the idea of being separate from others [the notion of a person], the idea that he is inferior [the notion of a sentient being], or the idea that he is superior [the notion of longevity], he cannot be called a bodhisattva whose practice is second only to that of a buddha."

The Bodhisattva's Degree of Practice

A bodhisattva is someone who is at a stage prior to becoming a buddha, and whose degree of practice is second only to that of a buddha. If, after delivering all sentient beings and eliminating all defilements and idle thoughts present within his mind, the bodhisattva (the person who is to become a buddha) has any ideas or notions about having delivered these beings, the result will be that he is unable to ascend to the buddha ground or to obtain liberation. For this reason, we must let go of all of the ideas and images of the four misleading concepts. Only by so doing can we become outstanding bodhisattvas.

The practice toward becoming a buddha can be described in a number of stages. First, there is the dimension of dissolving desire. This stage could be characterized as the desire-world-sentient-being minds from the four births of embryo, egg, moisture, and metamorphosis. After this is the stage of practice toward freeing oneself from the fixating mind.

The fixating mind becomes instilled through the habit of seeking to enjoy the things we like, or of loathing and shunning the things we dislike. This defilement can be characterized through the sentient-being minds of the world of form: those with and without form. The next stage involves a very subtle form of delusion in which the shadow of thought both is and is not present. These are the sentient-being minds of the formless world: those with thoughts, those without thoughts, and those neither with nor without thoughts. If we are to classify these minds into two principal types, there are the low-level sentient-being minds—defilements that linger at the level of desire and require a far greater amount of practice—and more advanced defilements, which come after these wild defilements become much clearer and involve various ideas about the presence or absence of good and bad values in our mind, along with evaluations of ourselves. These advanced defilements could be called the defilements of the four misleading concepts. Those unable to subdue the defilements associated with these thoughts cannot be called true bodhisattvas.

When we go outside on a clear, cloudless day, we see that objects cast shadows—shadows of buildings, shadows of trees along the road, shadows of people. Just as these shadows follow along with objects, all operations of the human mind possess other minds that follow along like shadows. These are the four misleading concepts: the "notion of self," the "notion of a person," the "notion of a sentient being," and the "notion of longevity." These shadows have no substance and are unnecessary. Even bodhisattvas who have performed profound mind-practice are shrouded in these shadows, which obscure their wisdom and leave their great capabilities and mind of mercy unable to issue forth. Only when we have rid ourselves of these fixating minds and four misleading concepts can we become utterly free individuals. Fixation turns us in a mistaken direction, and notions or misleading concepts leave us pursuing empty shadows.

Four Shadows That Follow the Bodhisattva

The "notion of self" refers to a thought that places oneself at the center of all things. "These are my thoughts," we say. "This is my perspective." It is a defilement in which we seek to judge all affairs in this world according to our own standards, such as our personal interests, and to act accordingly. This is the most difficult defilement to overcome. It may be called the "fundamental defilement."

The "notion of a person" consists of thoughts in which we try too much to distinguish what is ours and what belongs to others through the manifestations of the notion of self. "That is other," we think. "It belongs to you. That is your interest." Fundamentally, when we consider the endlessly cycling principle whereby the thing called "I" exists together with others, and that which we think of as "other" now can ultimately be beneficial for me and represent my interest, we can understand that there is no "I" and "other." Likewise, there is no "I" and "other" when we view them from the perspective of essential nature and consider the truth of the great self of the universe.

The "notion of a sentient being" refers to a sense of inferiority in which we disparage and despise ourselves as worthless, trifling beings that have failed to attain buddhahood.

The "notion of longevity" refers to a sense of superiority, such as believing that our lives are worth more than those of others, that we possess talents and have achieved awakening, or that we are much older and possess profound experience from our years.

As I have stated many times, becoming a buddha is not simply a matter of escaping a stage where desires flourish and we are unmoved by desires. There are four false defilements awaiting us, and so bodhisattvas must focus their commitment endlessly on eliminating them if they are to become truly free buddhas.

The sentient being is pickled in the brine of desire.

The bodhisattva wags his tail with his shadow.

We cross a mountain to find a mountain,

wc cross thc water to find a mist.

On the ground empty even of the buddha,

no shadow is cast.

CHAPTER IV

WHERE THE BUDDHA'S MIND DWELLS

Marvelous Practice Without Dwelling

That moonlight unmindful in a cold, empty sky.

The deluded person is busy looking for the moon in the water.

The clear-eyed person says to raise our head and look at the moon in the sky.

The serene mountains, streams, plants, and trees are filled with dharma flowers.

"Furthermore, Subhuti, the bodhisattva should perform acts of charity without being bound by the dharma. This is charity without dwelling in form, charity without dwelling on sound, smell, taste, touch, or ideas.

Subhuti, the bodhisattva should perform charity in this way, without dwelling on notions. For what reason must he do so?

When the bodhisattva performs acts of charity without dwelling on notions, the blessings and merits are immeasurable.

What do you think, Subhuti? Can you measure the expanse of the eastern space?"

"I cannot, World Honored One."

"Subhuti, can you measure the expanse of space to the south, west, or north, in the four directions between zenith and nadir?"

"I cannot, World Honored One."

"Subhuti, the merits of the bodhisattva performing acts of charity without dwelling on notions are similarly immeasurable. Subhuti, the bodhisattva should practice as I have taught."

Focus on

In answer to the question, "Where should we keep our mind?" the Buddha teaches in this section that if the bodhisattva abides in a mind free of misleading concepts, the resulting merits are without limit. As the person living the best of lives, how does the buddha carry his mind in daily life? Where should we be fixing our mind in our life? We will now learn about where we should be abiding with our mind and why the greatest merits come from lingering in the void-like mind.

"And Subhuti! The bodhisattva who performs profound mind-practice bestows the mind of mercy without being constrained by all things material and spiritual. For instance, he must use his mind without being captivated by all the colors visible to the eye, or the sounds, smells, tastes, tactile sensations, or ideas that come from outside.

"Subhuti! The bodhisattva must act from a place of utter freedom, one that is not captivated by ideas."

Where Should the Mind Linger?

I will explain in a bit more detail about the word *dharma*. In Buddhism, it is said that all objects are the dharma. The Buddha's instructions are said to be dharma, as are not only all the myriad material things but also the ideas carried within our minds. Mind-images are dharma, and so are material phenomena. In sum, *dharma* could be said to refer to all sensory conditions.

For this reason, the words "bestowing the mind of mercy without being constrained by all things material and spiritual" mean producing that mind without dwelling or fixating on any of these sensory conditions. To explain this in somewhat more detail, I will address the question of "where we should abide with our mind."

This question can be turned around to ask, "How should we use our mind?" or "What standard should we apply for our mind?" The Buddha's answer was that we should keep our mind in the void, and use our mind like the void.

Sentient beings possess ideas that sustain them. For instance, when desire takes the lead, we experience minds of poor discrimination or avarice. We are dominated in our lives by minds that declare, "I have a good heart," "I am attractive in this or that way," "I have outstanding talents," "I am from a noble family," and so on. In the presence of these minds, we experience anger when the place where we dwell is compromised by others, and, conversely, we experience pleasure when we are praised. When we dwell in some place, we find ourselves always being controlled from outside. Moreover, we compare our dwelling with those of other people, and our minds can never find peace because we are unable to free them from the other sensory conditions that are constantly entering from outside. Thus we need to examine ourselves, asking where our mind is principally fixated, and to move our mind away from its reliance on that fixation. Where should we move it? To a new address in the original mind that existed before our single mind emerged. That original mind is the mind of nirvana, the void mind, the no-mind.

Sentient beings dwell in desire, practitioners of the Way dwell in misleading concepts, and the buddha dwells nowhere. All of us will become buddhas when we change our dwelling in desire and concepts to dwelling in nothing.

What Is Charity?

Consider a piece of photographic film before any image emerges from the negative. We need to preserve a mind like that film. And if, at the next stage, we insist on having no thoughts at all, this corresponds to the mind without thoughts in terms of the nine sentient-being minds. We must therefore practice to have the no-mind when the no-mind is needed, and to being able to freely use mindfulness and the no-mind as is suitable for the affairs before us.

Achieving total liberation means dwelling in the void. This comes first, followed by dwelling without dwelling in the void, and then producing minds of charity upon this foundation.

We must understand these three stages if we are to effectively engage in dwelling without dwelling. The core of *The Diamond Sutra* is the teaching of "performing acts of service without any dwelling." Here, acts of service mean giving to others unconditionally and without notions of charity. Typically, we only perform charitable acts for people with whom we share affinities. A buddha, however, gives to all sentient beings when the opportunity arises , regardless of whether he shares affinities with them or not.

We should give thought today to whether we have caused harm to others in our life, and to whether living creatures have benefited from our presence. Each of us possesses a wealth of jewels that allow us to benefit others. One of these is our body, which we can use to relieve the travails of others. With our words, we can give hope to others. With our minds, we can offer mercy and warmth. We can help others with our riches. The person who is capable of helping others at every time and in every place, who knows how to give all he has to all living creatures, down to the smallest microbes and insects, could be called a bodhisattva or a buddha. All of you may perform charitable acts for your family members and your affinities. Those we esteem live for their country, and even greater esteem is given to those who live for all humankind. But the bodhisattva and the buddha perform charitable acts for all living creatures.

INTERPRETATION

"Why is this so? It is because when the bodhisattva performs acts of mercy without dwelling or fixation, the corresponding merits are without limit.

"Subhuti! Can you measure the expanse of the eastern sky, or of all the skies in the north, south, and west?"

"I cannot, World Honored One!"

"Subhuti! When the bodhisattva grants mercy without being bound to his obsessions and ideas, the merits will be as boundless as the void.

"Subhuti! As I have taught, the bodhisattva must carry his mind like the void."

The Merits of Freedom

We ordinary humans and sentient beings are always desire dwellers, with minds that linger in desire; pleasure dwellers, with minds that linger in the things that we enjoy; or notion dwellers, idealizing the notion that some truth exists even though none does, and dwelling within that image of the truth. In this way, we must bind our mind to something to put it at ease. Only once we have boldly severed these ties can we achieve liberation, transcendence and freedom.

When our mind is free of obstacles, we gain the wisdom to make the right judgments about objects. If the mind is free yet lacks wise judgments, then this is not true freedom, but merely self-indulgence. Freedom and wisdom will arise in the mind that has been trained to dwell nowhere. This is surely a great merit. Freedom, composure, and judgment cannot be purchased with any wealth or privilege, nor are they acquired from education and reading. This is the merit that emerges when we truly put into practice the Way of *The Diamond Sutra*.

Freedom and wisdom necessarily produce mercy. If one is wise yet produces no merciful love, then this is not true wisdom, but merely knowledge, or else false wisdom that may cause harm to others. By its nature, wisdom is accompanied by the mind of mercy, and the wise person necessarily performs acts of charity for those of his neighbors who are less fortunate. When we perform such acts of charitable merit, blessings and merits return to us from other people.

In other words, unlimited blessings and merits visit us because of our charitable merits.

Reader! Where is your mind lingering now? You must keep it in "the mind of here and now." What mind is it that I am teaching? It is ever present within you, and so you should not seek it somewhere far away, nor should you judge it too difficult and wait to see the nature. Find it right now, and linger in that mind. It is the home of the buddhas of the present, past, and future.

The Buddha says that merits without limit return to us when we perform many acts of charity with a mind that has no dwelling. I have provided an explanation about this, but I would like to elaborate here. The time when we have discovered the void-like diamond mind absent of all minds of desire, good and evil, and come to linger there, is the ultimate bliss. It is the peaceful bliss of nirvana. It is the home where the buddha dwells when he has no affairs to attend to. But when he does have affairs to attend to—when he encounters people and takes care of matters—he makes certain to perform acts of charity and mercy grounded in the principle of retribution and response of cause and effect. Both acts of charity and acts of mercy, however, are necessarily grounded in the void-like mind that has no dwelling. Buddhas and bodhisattvas make certain to take as their refuge the mind free of dwelling and to cultivate merits with the mind of mercy. Only when these two things are done do we become a buddha.

We live for the pleasure of satisfying desires.

We live with the pretension of being greater than others.

What will we do when we let go of enjoyment and pretensions?

The Buddha's great realization is a storm on the plain.

Give food when they are hungry and a pillow when they are tired.

The Buddha left no other words but this.

CHAPTER V

THE UNCHANGING REALITY

Truly Seeing the Principle of Suchness

Transactions at the market follow market rates.

Let us not be taken in by sweetly whispered words.

Sometimes, the mountains are water, and other times merely mountains.

Where does the void end on the day the fog lifts?

"Subhuti! What do you think? Can one recognize the Tathāgata through his bodily form?"

"No, World Honored One. The Tathāgata cannot be recognized through his bodily form. For the bodily form spoken of by the Tathāgata is not the bodily form."

Said the Buddha to Subhuti, "All that is with form is illusory. When you see that all form is not form, you will see the Tathāgata."

Focus on

This chapter teaches that when we realize with certainty that the shape of every object that we encounter is constantly changing and thus unreliable, we will encounter the true face of the tathāgata. A person's life is either agonizing or pleasant because he lives with attachment to the material things sensed from outside, without attention to the use of his mind. In other words, the material world treats sentient beings like playthings. Yet those material things upon which we fixate are constantly changing phantoms. We open our eyes to the truth when we realize their phantom nature. In this chapter, we will learn about practice toward awakening to the unchanging mind.

"Subhuti! Can you see the tathāgata that is the truth-mind through the sacred body of the Buddha [bodily form]?"

"No, World Honored One! Even the majestic body of which you speak is not eternal but changing. I cannot see the tathāgata through the body."

The Marvelous Appearance of the Buddha

Generally, the founders of religions are born possessing marvelous bodies and attractive features. Because ordinary sentient beings scrutinize appearance before seeing character or use of the mind, the earliest leaders of a religion come to possess appearances outstanding enough to focus people's attention. It appears that the Buddha possessed an even more marvelous appearance than other sages. As a result, the students who believed in and followed him may have succumbed to the misapprehension that a person was a buddha because he had an attractive appearance. They may have also gone farther and identified the tathāgata, that is the truth mind, with the appearance of the buddha. Because of this, the Buddha provides explicit instruction as to the difference between appearance and the tathāgata realm.

The attractive face of the Buddha is another phenomenon,

and as such it is subject to change. Even with the character of a buddha, appearance may ultimately manifest itself in different forms according to the circumstances. Moreover, we are obliged to consider an even more fundamental problem: explaining how the buddha came to be, or explaining the truth nature of the tathāgata that was revealed consistently in the buddha's mind. This nature is both a root and an eternal text for all the buddhas and sages. There exists a principle that governs all the myriad natural phenomena in the universe. Minds are constantly changing—emotions of joy, anger, sorrow, and pleasure intertwine—and behind all these phenomena exists the truth of the tathāgata. We must not make the mistake of identifying this tathāgata, the mind of true suchness, with an attractive face.

Understanding the tathāgata truth mind of the Buddha, Subhuti says that however attractive one's countenance may be, that body is not the same as the Dharmakāya, which is the body of the dharma. In other words, a phenomenon, whatever its value, is different from a truth being.

"Subhuti! All beings both with and without shape are illusory, without any substance to them.

When you understand that the myriad phenomena of the universe are not the reality, you will immediately see the buddha that, being just as it is, is like the void."

The Mind-ground Revealed When the Leaves of Defilement Fall Away

A four-line gatha is a dharma instruction on the truth in the form of a song. Here, we must understand the essential mind, the original mind. Before, when asked how to subdue the mind, the Buddha answered that we must awaken to the tathāgata mind and dissolve the defilements with an undefiled mind, and when asked where our mind should abide, he said that we must keep our mind in the tathāgata realm that is eternally unchanging, without beginning or end, without addition or subtraction. In this chapter, we will need to awaken with certainty to the buddha mind.

Everything phenomenal on the outside is illusory, ceaselessly changing. Money, honors, power, you and I—all of it is changing into different illusory aspects at every moment. In a sense, it is as though we are riding on a constantly changing train. Our minds, too, are constantly changing. At one time, we may find a certain type of person pleasant, yet as the years pass we come to like another type of person. The foods that we enjoy likewise change, as do our causes and principles. If the entities on the outside can be termed "object notions," then what happens inside our minds could be called "mind notions," but both object notions and mind notions are equally illusory. People live their lives being deceived by illusory objects and mind notions. The grass and trees that flourished in the spring and summer fall away and scatter on the ground when the autumn comes. The unchanging ground, however, is eternal. All the different minds arise and vanish. Where are thoughts born, and where do they return? What kind of mind exists before the emergence of thoughts?

René Descartes said, "I think, therefore I am." But where did thought emerge? There exists a mind-ground from which thoughts emerge. This is sometimes called "tathāgata," and sometimes called "Dharmakāya." Hear and absorb this great news.

How difficult, how very difficult.
The more you seek, the farther it recedes.
How simple, how very simple.
The more you release it, the more clearly it is revealed.
Ha ha, ho ho.

CHAPTER VI

PROPHECIES ON THE DHARMA-ENDING WORLD

The Rarity of Right Belief

So beautiful, the meeting on Vulture Peak.
The dharma seat is all the warmer with the moonlight shining.
In his fixation, he worries about the end times.
Tsk tsk, Subhuti. The sun rises when the moon sets.

Subhuti asked the Buddha, "World Honored One! With there exist a sentient being who will hear these words that you have spoken and produce sincere faith?"

Said the Buddha to Subhuti, "Do not say such things. In the last five hundred years after the Tathāgata's nirvana, there will be one who upholds the precepts and cultivates blessings, and he will produce the mind of faith at these words and take them as truth. You must understand this.

This person will be one who has sown seeds of goodness not under one or two, three or four, or five buddhas alone, but in the presence of innumerable tens of millions of buddhas, and thus he will have produced a pure mind of faith in just a single thought upon hearing these words.

Subhuti! The Tathāgata sees and knows all. All these sentient beings will attain such limitless merits. For all these sentient beings do not harbor conceptions of the self, the person, the sentient being, or long life, the dharma notion, or the notion that is not dharma.

Why is this so? If any of these sentient beings adopts a notion in his mind, he will fixate on conceptions of the self, the person, the sentient being, and long life.

Why is this so? If he adopts the dharma notion, he will fixate on conceptions of the self, the person, the sentient being, and long life, and if he adopts the notion that is not dharma, he will fixate on conceptions of the self, the person, the sentient being, and long life.

For this reason, he should not adopt the dharma or the non-dharma. In this sense, as the Tathāgata always says, you bhikṣus understand that my teachings are like a raft. The dharma should be released as a matter of course. So much more should that which is not dharma be released."

Focus on

Hearing the Buddha's endlessly profound *Diamond Sutra*, Subhuti remarks that those present have heard and awakened to the wisdom of it themselves, but worries what will happen when the end times come. How, he asks, will the practitioners of that age produce minds of faith having only known the scripture through the written word? In response, the Buddha prophesies that there will exist someone who believes in and practices the notionless truth even in the end times, and that this person will be a special student of Buddhism who has sown seeds of goodness in many buddha orders in previous lives. In this chapter, we will consider what kind of age the end times will be, and the nature of the practices of those who are dedicated to the cultivation of the Way.

Said Subhuti to the Buddha, "In the distant future, when you are not here, will the sentient beings hear the dharma instruction on notionless mind-practice and produce minds of faith as we do here today?"

Said the Buddha to Subhuti, "Do not worry so. Even 2,500 years after the Tathāgata's nirvana, there will be one who upholds the precepts and accumulates blessings, someone who produces a true mind of faith toward the truth without form and sincerely puts it into practice. You must understand this. It will be someone who has observed innumerable buddhas in previous lives and sown many, many seeds of goodness, not only seeds for one or two buddhas. Only such a person will hear the unsurpassed dharma instruction and produce a pure mind of faith."

Subhuti's Worries about the End Times

It may be the case that Subhuti, like the other listeners, was profoundly impressed to hear the Buddha's response to his question about subduing mistaken minds and his interpretation of the place where the mind is kept. Now, he asks about the fate of sentient beings in the very distant future. The people present are hearing the Buddha speak directly, and thus being guided on the path of practice. But in the future, the Buddha will not be there. How, then, will sentient beings receive his profound dharma instructions? In other words, Subhuti is asking, "How will sentient beings awaken to the buddhadharma and practice when the end times come and the Buddha is not there?"

The reader must understand that a new sage will unquestionably emerge in the end times. In Chinese history, the Spring and Autumn Period and the Warring States Period are described as the most turbulent of times. It was during this time that Confucius emerged with his new philosophical movement, giving hope and edification to the public. Indeed, the time when the Buddha emerged in India was also a turbulent age, and it could also be said that the period that saw the emergence of Jesus Christ was a tremendously trying era. It was at just such a time that Jesus emerged with his evangelical movement. It appears that Subhuti lacked the awareness of historical change that would come several millennia later.

Reader! What age are we living in today? It is one of rapid, revolutionary change. Without question, we are living in turbulent times, times of crisis. We must believe with certainty that at such a time, a new sage will emerge to save the world with a doctrine suited to the world of the future.

This time can be understood in terms of the "last five hundred years after the Tathāgata's *nirvana*." The times after the Buddha are divided into the "period of the orthodoxy and vigor," "the period of semblance," and "the period of decline and termination." The first of these is seen as a period of around 500 years, during which the buddhadharma thrived. The second is described as a peripheral time, a period of one thousand years that witnessed outstanding interpretations and the production of much writing. This period has also been called the "era of doctrinal writing." The next thousand years sees a transition into a period of decline and termination, and is called the "age of formal and solemn Buddhism." Thus are the 2,500 years described.

Buddhists Who Uphold Precepts Inwardly and Create Blessings Outwardly

Consider those who uphold the precepts and create blessings. All religions have negative precepts—that is to say, taboos. Nations, too, have their prohibitions. A taboo means that a certain act torments the perpetrator, harms others, and wreaks havoc on society. A child who has not yet attained wisdom cannot distinguish this clearly. Once we have reached adulthood, however, we become aware of the things that we must do and the things that we must not do. But the person who becomes the founder of a religion takes this to a higher level and encourages his followers to uphold precepts in order to forestall things that are fundamentally harmful to the human heart, that could lead to punishment in the distant future, and that cause great harm to society and one's neighbors. Such precepts are difficult to uphold. When we do so, however, we break free from our dissolute way of living and gain true freedom. Accepting these precepts in our minds, and upholding them, are acts of faith and practice.

To abide by precepts means to abide with the buddha. It could be said that the observance of precepts is the foundation that ennobles a person's character. Moreover, it is a shortcut to freeing oneself from transgressions and evil. If you visit a harbor, you will see the breakwaters built to block the crashing waves. The breakwater is intended to resist the force of the waves. Observance of precepts will serve as a breakwater that shields us from the waves of transgressions, evil and temptation.

Next, there is the creation of blessings. People today often use the expressions, "Luck is with me," or "Luck is against me." Why should this be? We say these things because we do not understand that our fortune is the result of our receiving rewards today for having helped others in our previous lives. We talk about good luck and blessings because we do not understand about previous lives. Conversely, the person who has harmed and caused damage to others often finds himself lucklessly enduring hardship no matter how hard he works. This is called "receiving as we have created"— our recompense for the karma that we have made for ourselves.

Every religion encourages its followers to help their neighbors and benefit society with a kind heart. It asks us to enrich society, to create a community of harmonious relationships, and to cultivate happy lives for ourselves.

The Buddha said that even amid the turbulence of the end times, there will unquestionably be someone who engages in the mind-practice without form—which could be called the greatest of all practice—and experiences the ultimate bliss. It will be someone who has created blessings and fervently upheld the precepts over the course of many previous lives.

Are you committing yourself sincerely to upholding the Buddha's precepts? Are you putting good works into practice for the sake of others and society?

These two types of practice constitute the basic framework for creating our character. Internal truth is ultimately formed through precepts, and the happiness of receiving the help of others is the outcome of our having helped others.

> Śākyamuni carried on the mantle of Dīpaṃkara Buddha.
> Confucius carried Yao and Shun on his back.
> Jesus held Abraham at his breast.
> These days, foolish enlightened ones noisily proclaim
> "I am the greatest."
> A lifetime of faith by sentient beings becomes etched in stone.
> The sage before, the sage after—their belief
> and dedication are boundless.

"Subhuti! The Tathāgata sees and knows all about how his students come and go in their eternal lives. Those who are devout in their belief and dedication will enjoy boundless blessings and merits in the future, for such people commit themselves sincerely to eliminating the four misleading concepts, the dharma notion, and even the non-dharma notion."

The Stages of the Buddha's Students

There exist certain stages that people pass through as they are being saved by a buddha or religion. First, there is one of forming an affinity. In this stage, we hear the wonderful news of the Buddha and develop a vague sense of admiration and appreciation for him. We are learning of the great physician who will cure our ills and begin forming a close relationship with him.

Next, there is the stage in which we hear of the wondrousness of the Buddha and receive personal instruction, putting his teachings into practice and seeking to join in his will. We might call this the stage of belief and dedication. In this stage we hear the doctor's prescription for curing our ailment, we take our medicine, and receive treatment.

After that comes the stage of practice, when we put the Buddha's dharma instruction into practice ourselves. Where the belief and dedication stage sees us depending upon the virtue and authority of the Buddha's words and achieving salvation through the power of others, the practice stage sees us becoming subjects in our own right, putting the Buddha's dharma into practice and experiencing it for ourselves—a stage of practice where we are capable of diagnosing our own ailment and finding the proper prescription even when the Buddha is far from us.

The practitioner in the third stage is not one who has formed an affinity with the Buddha in a single lifetime. Rather, it is someone who has fervently practiced while moving between the stages of Buddha affinity, belief and dedication, and practice at the bosom of sages, and under their dharma, over the course of a great many previous lives.

The person who has performed this practice will not be swayed by the waves of temptation and hardship of a turbulent world in the end times. There will arise in him a perfect mind of faith, such that he hears the correct doctrine and says, "This dharma is exactly the religion I was looking for." With this mind of faith, he will engage in a higher level of mind-practice.

The Powers of a Buddha

Buddhas possess a variety of powers and miraculous abilities. One of these is the power of transcendent wisdom. This means the ability to master and understand everything. We have no way of understanding the changes of the world, nor can we know of things to come many thousands of years hence. We do not know if someone is in a period of progression or regression. We do not know if a group is proceeding downhill or uphill. The Buddha's insight, however, is a penetrating perspective the likes of which we cannot imagine—the ability to understand all things.

In this chapter, the Buddha himself says that he sees and knows the minds and actions of his believing followers. Since sentient beings would be fearful of facing a buddha who declared that he knows all about their minds, there would likely be many occasions in which a buddha feigned ignorance, despite his knowledge.

Yet he explicitly says here that he knows and sees all. I suspect he may have said this as a kind of warning. "All of you are students engaged in high-level practice," he is saying. "Do you also have this kind of ability? You must not content yourselves with your current practice, but exert yourselves further and reach a higher level of wisdom." The mind-practice that we perform equips us with limitless capabilities and wisdom.

I will share an old verse with which all of you are familiar. I hope you will use it for assessment in your mind-practice.

"However high the great mountain may be,

it is still a mountain under the sky.

There is none who cannot climb it if he keeps moving upward.

But not all climb it—they merely say the mountain is high."

INTERPRETATION

"I tell you this at every opportunity. I have likened the dharma that I preach to a ferryboat that you monks should use only when crossing the river. So if you abandon the dharma, still less is there any need to be bound to something that is not even dharma.

"Those engaged in this mind-practice without notion do not seek to hold the dharma or the non-dharma, for they know why they are controlled by the four misleading concepts if there should be even the slightest notion obstructing their mind, and why they are ensnared by the four misleading concepts at the foundation of samsara if there is even a trace of dharma or non-dharma notions."

Do Not Fixate Even on the Buddhadharma

When we first engage in mind-practice toward becoming a buddha, we learn to take the doctrines taught by the Buddha as our compass, to devote our lives according to the teaching, and to abide by its rules. In the next stage, we awaken to the truth at the foundation of the teaching. We then practice intently with this truth as our scripture. Truth exists in the mind; our own mind becomes the teacher that instructs us. When we practice in this way, we gain formidable abilities and acquire wisdom. At this point, we could be said to become outstanding individuals and sages.

The next stage sees us honing our ability to shed all the constraints of doctrine and the dharma in our mind and to be free and unrestricted. This is the no-mind stage in which we are free from the dharma, and the stage of the able mind in which we produce the right mind for any given time or place. The person practicing in this no-mind and able-mind stage must abandon the raft of the doctrine taught by the Buddha. But it is the commission of a transgression, and a corruption of the self, for someone who has not arrived at this state to take the buddhadharma as a raft. I hope there will be no misunderstanding here.

The message is that we must not live carrying notions in our mind. This is a repeated plea. A dharma master once said, "So tenaciously do notions follow us around that even a buddha has buddha notions. The buddha is simply capable of erasing them immediately and is thus not darkened by them." In other words, if we are not cautious about eliminating notions simply because we have a little bit of practice under our belt, we are immediately darkened by them. As these words state, all of us carry notions around in our lives. Thus we are entreated to engage in constant practice toward freeing ourselves from them.

The "dharma notion" refers to our own idea that we are doing a good job of putting the teachings of the Buddha into practice. The "non-dharma notion," in contrast, refers to our pride in having escaped a sense of pride about putting the teachings of the Buddha into practice. This means that we have a false perception about absence.

Among the nine categories of sentient beings, those with and without thoughts and those neither with nor without thoughts fall into this category. When you go to a temple, you will see what is called the "Arhat Hall." These Arhats are proficient at one aspect of practice, and they seek to serve only one buddha in their affinities. They have abilities even greater than the buddha's in terms of one particular direction. Yet they lack the ability to do all things equally, and so they are honored in the Arhat Hall. If we are unwittingly ensnared by false ideas of dharma, we may gain abilities from our practice, but we will end up being enshrined in the Arhat Hall. And even when we have subdued mistaken minds, we must be able to free ourselves with certainty from notions, or else our wisdom will be darkened, as we are shrouded in still another self-shadow. Our abilities will become fixed in one direction, so that we become the half-enlightened, forever unable to become presiding sages.

Where should the sentient being attach itself
to find peace of mind?
The novice enlightened one takes as a root
the notions of good seeds.
The white cloud provides no prop,
and so he plays with various faces.
The buddha has nothing even to let go of,
and so he grasps the heavens and earth.

CHAPTER VII

GROUNDING IN
THE NO-MIND
Nothing Attained, Nothing Taught

Ah! It is said in words that it cannot be put in words.

A rueful smile at a single, slender flower.

Yang Guifei calling vainly for Little Jade.

The wise one says the interpretation is better than the dream.

"Subhuti, What do you think? Has the Tathāgata has obtained Anuttara-Samyak-Sambodhi? Has the Tathāgata taught a dharma?"

Said Subhuti, "As I have understood the Buddha's words, the name of 'Anuttara-Samyak-Sambodhi' is given to that which has no fixed dharma, and the Tathāgata taught that there is no fixed dharma.

The dharma cannot be possessed completely, nor can it be expressed in words. It is not a dharma, yet is not a non-dharma. Why is this so? It is because all of the sages and wise ones have allowed discrimination to be through this unconditioned dharma."

Focus on

In this section, we are taught that the unsurpassed great truth, the highest truth that we practitioners of the Way are seeking to awaken to and practice, is not a dharma restricted to any particular thing, and that it cannot be held or expressed in words. Here we will learn what kind of mind this great truth is, and what sort of discrimination dharma we should produce based on the dharma of no-action.

"Subhuti! Do you believe that the Tathāgata has obtained the unsurpassed great truth, or that there is a dharma taught by the Tathāgata?"

Said Subhuti, "As I have understood your words, I have given that which has no fixed dharma the name of 'unsurpassed great path,' and I believe the Tathāgata spoke of dharma that originally has no dharma."

The True Mind Is Neither Loving Nor Hateful

What kind of thing, what kind of mind, is the dharma that is not fixed? With loving minds and hateful minds, agonizing and pleasant minds, it is possible to express the state of mind in words or writing. Yet our original mind, which we are incapable of saying exists or does not exist, cannot be conceptualized as some thing, nor can it be given a particular form. The Buddha called this mind "tathāgata," and he also used the term without fixed dharma" here.

The Founding Master called this the perfect and complete mind—a mind endowed with all kinds of capabilities. He also said that it is a mind of supreme tranquility, with all means of linguistic expression severed, and a mind that transcends all "existence" or "nonexistence." In the opening chapter of the *Daodejing*, Laotze said that the Way that can be called "the Way" is not the true Way (道可道非常道).

Long ago, there was a monk named Xuefeng. He saw some monkeys playing and said, "Each of those monkeys is playing with its own ancient mirror."

Hearing this, a monk named Sansheng said, "Over all the years, that ancient mirror had no name, and now you call it 'ancient mirror'?"

At which Xuefeng said, "Oh, no. It is scratched now."

Each person carries his own mirror. It makes him observe, think, laugh, and speak. All of you are reading my lecture now, but what exists such that you see it? Some will say that our eyes are seeing it. You see the words of my lecture because you have a mind-mirror. What is the most suitable name for this mind-mirror with no face? The Buddha says that it is "without fixed dharma."

INTERPRETATION

"For the dharma of which the Tathāgata spoke cannot be possessed by anyone, nor can it be expressed in words. It is a dharma with no dharma, yet is not not a dharma. Thus all of the sages and wise ones produce and cull discriminating minds based on this dharma of no-action."

The Buddha's Standards for Discrimination

The dharma of no-action is an infinite mind, one that cannot be defined as any one thing or trapped in any framework. This infinite mind is called the "essential nature" and the "foundation." Discernment by producing the proper discrimination for any object when we encounter sensory conditions while remaining grounded in this infinite mind is called "allowing discrimination to be." In the Confucian concept of the Doctrine of the Mean, the "center" (*zhong*, 中) was said to be what exists prior to the emergence of feelings of joy and anger, sorrow and pleasure, and the term "harmony" (*he*, 和) described the production of the right mind for moderation within this center. Thus the doctrine of no-action corresponds to the center in the Doctrine of the Mean, and "allowing discrimination to be" corresponds to harmony.

When parents love their children, it is realistically impossible for them to do so in the same way at all times. When a child suffers misfortune, they will first feel minds of pity and love for him. At another time, their minds will go to the child who listens well. Discriminations are made in this way, but discriminations are not necessarily bad. There may not be any discrimination when we divide money equally among our children, but it is right and fair to divide it according to their situations. We are only capable of seeing fairly and making the right discrimination for the circumstances when we are grounded in the realm of nonbeing.

The Buddha has a standard for discrimination, namely cause and effect. He adopts the standard of the principle of retribution and response of cause and effect, and he uses that as a measure in his discriminations. Ultimately, buddhas discriminate according to the standard of cause and effect from the realm of nonbeing. If we compare this to the *Dharma of Timeless Sŏn* in *Won*-Buddhism, it could be said that the words "take true voidness as the substance" become "take the dharma of no-action as the substance," while the words "[take] marvelous existence as the function" become "discriminate all things with marvelous existence as a standard."

In the mind-practice of practitioners of the Way in the three periods, awakening to and practicing the doctrine of no-action has been relatively easy, but actually producing the proper discriminating mind for each different sensory condition and handling affairs successfully has been difficult. Thus, when the level of one's practice increases, the simple approach is to ground it in the doctrine of no-action at all times, and it becomes very difficult and constantly demanding to give the proper buddha offerings suited to each situation.

On one occasion, the Founding Master scolded a student very sternly. Later, a student came to see him and worried about possibly being upbraided as well. Unexpectedly, that fearsome face that had just delivered a stern reprimand immediately became peaceful and merciful, and the Founding Master treated this student warmly. This is an example of producing the right discriminating mind grounded in an effortless state of mind, reprimanding one and praising another according to the person and the circumstances.

In Pyeongyang, they entertain guests with only cold noodles.
Deshan enlightened visiting monks by striking them with a cudgel.
The Dharmakāya nurtures all things through the four seasons.
Mt. Namsan stands here, the Hangang River flows that way.

CHAPTER VIII

THE TRUE BUDDHADHARMA REQUIRES ABANDONING THE BUDDHADHARMA

Being Born from Reliance on the Dharma

You cannot make rice with sand.
Day after day, people wash the grains of sand.
In his mercy, the Buddha said the obvious,
Ah, food can only be made with rice.

"Subhuti! What do you think? If a person performs charitable acts for others with enough seven treasures to fill the Three Thousand Great Thousand Worlds, would you say that this person will definitely gain many blessings and merits?"

Said Subhuti, "Very many, World Honored One! For these blessings and merits are not the source of blessings and merits, and thus the Tathāgata taught that the blessing and merits are many."

"If some other person were to accept and uphold even the four-line gatha from this sutra and speak it to others, the resulting blessings and merits would exceed even those."

For Subhuti! For all the buddhas and their teachings on Anuttara-Samyak-Sambodhi emerge from this sutra.

Subhuti! That which is called by the name of 'buddhadharma' is not the buddhadharma."

Focus on

The standards for practice for all buddhas and practitioners of the Way come from *The Diamond Sutra*. In this chapter, however, the Buddha says that buddhadharma in the true sense (*The Diamond Sutra*) must not be bound to the concept of the buddhadharma, or have any obstruction. Here, we will learn the difference between the blessings and merits obtained through charitably giving material things to others and the merits of awakening to the teachings of *The Diamond Sutra* and teaching them to others, and we will attempt to awaken to the original mind that is called the source of *The Diamond Sutra*.

"Subhuti! What do you think? Can you say that a person who performs charitable acts for others with the seven treasures that fill the universe will obtain many blessings and merits?

Said Subhuti, "Very many, World Honored One! But because these blessings and merits not the source of blessings and merits, their number would be such that not even the Buddha could count them. It may be said that if some other person were to practice the supreme way that is the four-line gatha, which may be called the core of *The Diamond Sutra*, and to communicate this to others, the blessings and merits would be far greater than those from giving the seven treasures of gold, silver, lapis, crystal, coral, agate, and pearls."

Find the Source That Enriches Material Things

In the course of a person's life, the power of material things assumes tremendous significance. Within the capitalist society in particular, economic might serves as a means of evaluating people.

In this chapter, the Buddha declares unequivocally that even if someone possesses enough of the seven treasures to fill the universe and gives correspondingly to others, such economic wealth cannot, in the end, bring a person happiness. What, then, would be capable of doing so? The answer, Buddha taught, is that the person who has awakened to and come to possess the mind-ground can enjoy the greatest happiness and value.

To begin with, material abundance, however much we may spend, has a limit because it is tangible. Furthermore, when we wrap ourselves in material wealth and indulge our desires, we become corrupt and arrogant and suffer the pains of samsara. Ultimately, we find ourselves drifting farther away from the sacred values, which may be called the absolute values.

Let us think for a moment about where material abundance comes from. When a person accumulates material and economic wealth, this mind is not the first thing to arise. Perhaps a seed of envy toward another's riches is first to sprout, which create to a firm resolution to acquire wealth. In this way, a person comes to possess a mind of diligence, a mind toward saving, a mind toward restraint, a mind of sincere commitment to money. Ultimately, it is the mind that leads to the accumulation of material wealth. To consider the question more deeply, where do these different, marvelous minds come from, the marvelous thoughts that drive one to earn this money? The marvelous seeds of good emerged from the mind-ground that all of us possess, the truth-nature of the mind. Here, the truth-nature of the mind was referred to as the "source of blessings and merits."

The reason that all of us can enjoy material abundance if we keep working toward it ultimately has to do with the source of blessings and merits. Ordinary sentient beings, however, do not understand or concern themselves with the principles of the mind as they pursue the phenomenal, limited things of the material world. In the process, they become slaves to these things and suffer unhappiness.

Because we lose our minds from our absorption in material things—which might be called the "end of value"—we should not pursue material abundance alone, but strive for the truth-nature of the mind that is its basis, the principle of the mind's functioning. When we do so, we can enjoy material abundance, we gain the power to freely operate those material things, and, when we develop our source of blessings and merits, we can enjoy ultimate and heavenly bliss the likes of which we can never know or experience through material abundance—a bliss that allows us to escape from all torment.

We have awakened to the fact that the way to help the poor and hungry overcome poverty forever is not to give them tens of thousands of loaves of bread, but to teach them how to make bread, and that the act of teaching that method is a far greater merit than giving tens of thousands of loaves.

"Yes, Subhuti! For the teachings of all buddhas and the unsurpassed great path emerged from this *Diamond Sutra*.

"But Subhuti! The true buddhadharma can never be when one is bound to the *Diamond Sutra* way that is called by the name of buddhadharma."

The Scriptures Were Created by the Mind, But What Kind of Mind?

All of the presiding sages who formed the great religions in human history awakened to the truth. They also predicted what would come in the future, establishing doctrines suited to the society of the future world and teaching these to their followers.

Of all of these teachings, *The Diamond Sutra* could be called the text with the greatest spiritual capacity for practitioners. When we strive to accept and carry its content, to read and recite it, and thus to achieve awakening and put it into practice, we can become teachers of humankind like the Buddha. It may be said of such a person that he lives the greatest of lives, and he may live that life amid a feeling of true happiness at every moment.

If we consider whether the many great students of the Buddha would have become high-level sages like the Buddha had they not taken *The Diamond Sutra* as their text, we will realize that we truly owe that sutra a myriad of bows. Let us consider, though, the picture that *The Diamond Sutra* paints for us, the thing to which its finger points. Words and language necessarily have meaning as guides pointing to something, and are not the thing itself. The word "money" denotes the concept of money, but it is not actual money. Reader, the person of great spiritual capacity who is capable of truly reading the truth contained in *The Diamond Sutra* will practice choosing and instilling the blessing nature pointed to by the words. And those with even greater capacity will not be trapped or impeded by the blessing nature, but will become truly free individuals who are not bound to anything—even the buddhadharma. Reader, what mind is it that *The Diamond Sutra* illuminates? Try to picture this.

Emerging from desire, they are defilements and idle thoughts.
Emerging from the public spirit, it is said to be just.
Whence will it emerge when it is called *The Diamond Sutra*?
Buddhist, what is the difference between
the translation and the original?

CHAPTER IX

FOUR STAGES OF MIND-PRACTICE
The One Form Not Being Form

My Way, he said, is penetrated by a single thread.

Nature is so beautiful in all its layers.

The sound of the bamboo forest sweeping the void each night.

So the sky is blue and the stars shine.

"Subhuti! What do you think? Does the Stream-entrant [Srotāpanna] have the thought, 'I have obtained the fruit of the Stream-entrant?'"

"No, World Honored One!" said Subhuti. "For while the name 'Stream-entrant' means that he has entered the stream of the sage, he has not entered anything. He does not allow himself to be tainted by form, sound, smell, taste, touch, or ideas, and thus he is called by the name of 'Stream-entrant.'"

"Subhuti! What do you think? Does the Once-to-be-reborn [Sakṛdāgāmi] have the thought, 'I have obtained the fruit of the Once-to-be-reborn?'"

"No, World Honored One!" said Subhuti. "For while the name 'Once-to-be-reborn' means that he comes and goes once, there is in truth no coming or going, and thus he is called by the name of 'Once-to-be-reborn.'"

"Subhuti! What do you think? Does the Non-returner [Anāgāmi] have the thought, "I have obtained the fruit of the Non-returner?'"

"No, World Honored One!" said Subhuti. "For while the name 'Non-returner' [he who has at most one more lifetime in a celestial pure abode] means that he does not come, there is in truth no not-coming, and thus he is called by the name of 'Non-returner.'"

"Subhuti! What do you think? Does the Arhat have the thought, 'I have achieved the Way of the Arhat?'"

"No, World Honored One!" answered Subhuti. "For if the 'Arhat' has the thought, 'I have obtained the Way of the Arhat,' he has become fixated on conceptions of the self, the person, the sentient being, and long life.

World Honored One! The Buddha has said that I am foremost among those who have achieved samādhi without conflict and that I am an Arhat who is foremost in having separated from desires, but I do not have the thought, 'I am an Arhat who has separated from desires.'

"World Honored One, were I to have the thought, 'I have achieved the Way of the Arhat,' the World Honored One would not say, 'Subhuti is one who enjoys the practice of Aranya [without conflict].

But in truth Subhuti does not practice anything, and thus you have given him the name of 'one who enjoys the practice of Aranya.'"

Focus on

Four stages of practice are given for the greatest mind-practice, that of eliminating false notions in order to experience and internalize the highest truth. It could be said that the stages of practice presented here refer to cultivating the spirit because this was a time focused on cultivating the spirit. These four stages are also called the "four stages of Theravāda (Teachings of the Elders) practice." I hope that you will compare your own practice against the four mind stages described here.

"Subhuti! What do you think? Does the Stream-entrant boast of having performed practice enough to become a Stream-entrant?"

"No, World Honored One!" said Subhuti.

"For while the Stream-entrant has entered the ranks of the sages, he does not allow himself to be seduced by the thought of having joined them.

The name 'Stream-entrant' describes a level where one is not tainted by the six sensory conditions of color, sound, smell, taste, touch, and thought."

The Bodhisattva Who Has Reached the First Realm of Sagehood

Previously, Subhuti asked, "How are we to subdue wicked minds?" The Buddha described all of the wicked minds of sentient beings in terms of nine types and offered two methods for subduing them. The first involved making a firm vow to take responsibility for and deliver all sentient beings, and to eliminate any delusion of greed that arises by assessing it against the vow to become a buddha. In the second method, he taught that we could subdue any mistaken minds that emerge by assessing them against the self-nature, the original nature, since there are no delusions of desire in the realm of our original mind.

When we engage in continued practice toward subduing minds through assessing our vows and our self-nature, the Buddha tells us, the result will take the form of four stages according to the level of our sincerity.

Persons who read this passage will only become engaged in true practice when they compare it to their own level of practice, rather than disregarding it as a matter concerning others.

The Stream-entrant is a person who has practiced enough to subdue desires. Within a person's mind, the flames of greed are ceaselessly burning. We call this "instinct"—things like appetite, lust, material desires, sloth, or the desire for honors.

It cannot be said that such desires are necessarily bad. They are like crude oil—when properly refined, they transform into the most amazing substances. We can think of the process of cultivating the Way as one of refining our fundamental desires and instilling the ability to use them in marvelous ways. If we fail to tame these fundamental desires, however, they may turn into things that destroy us and cause harm to society and our neighbors. These instincts are like black clouds in the sky, darkening our wisdom and causing us to live in an animalistic way.

When, as mentioned before, we engage in practice toward overcoming desires by repeatedly assessing them against our self-nature and our vow, we must make the first stage one of unconditionally regarding the desires as Māra or demons and striving to overcome them. We must put every ounce of our strength into practice toward ridding ourselves of the Māra, without ever letting go of the spirit of a battle to the last. Otherwise, we will be controlled by the Māra and find ourselves unable to ever escape from the realm of desire.

Each person derives different pleasures from this life and past lives, and so the particular manifestations of the Māra may differ. One person may have a great desire for fortune, another gluttonous desires, another sexual lust, another sloth, and another a thirst for honors. Each must determine his own Māra and practice the right method for it. He must also be mindful of the sequence, first keeping such external temptations away and then overcoming them within sensory conditions.

This chapter mentions six types of sensory conditions. When the seeds of desire linger in our minds and we encounter the six sensory conditions from outside—the things that we see, hear, smell, taste, touch, and enjoy in our mind—the desires within our mind rise like flames in response to those conditions. This can certainly be conquered when we cultivate the Way, whether by restraining them so that they cannot arise or by sublimating them into high-level desires.

When we subdue our desire, we proceed from the category of "ordinary human and sentient being" to the category of "very beginner-level sage." The Stream-entrant falls into this category of sage or enlightened one.

The Stream-entrant is also called the "counter current." Generally, people in this world go with the flow toward the satisfaction of their desires. For instance, we celebrate becoming very rich, and we delight when great honors come our way. This is the general current of the world. The Stream-entrant, however, has not merged with these worldly waves of desire, but has swum against the current of desire and overcome it.

Reader, are you tainted by desire and drifting along on its waves without knowing it? Or are you working to dilute the waters of desire? Has the water level dropped enough that you are now turning away from the desiring mind and living within the realm of original nature as your master? Please scrutinize yourself.

While it is somewhat difficult to compare these stages with the dharma ranks in *Won*-Buddhism, if we do so we will see that the Stream-entrant has ascended to around the level of Māra defeated. The status of dharma strong and Māra defeated is a stage where, while one is not entirely free of desires and the four misleading concepts in one's mind, these have forfeited sovereignty and are restrained by the good mind. Should the person who has ascended to Stream-entrant rank let down his guard, he will sacrifice his sovereignty to desire. He must therefore work diligently to perform practice and accumulate merits, gathering strength so that his good mind always reigns supreme.

The sentient being flows downward on the waters of the desire river.

The Stream-entrant travels upstream, beating against the current.

You who are traveling the opposing road, keep going and do not stop.

Once you pass the ridge,

right there is the village of the buddha ground.

"Subhuti! What do you think?

Does the Once-to-be-reborn boast of having practiced enough to be a Once-to-be-reborn?"

Said Subhuti, "No, World Honored One!

For while the Once-to-be-reborn is at a level where he will come and go only once with sensory conditions, he has, in truth, no notion of possessing the practice ability for the single return. This is the level of practice that earns one the name of 'Once-to-be-reborn.'"

Sometimes the Shadow of Desire Comes and Goes

The embers of desire are not totally absent from the mind of the practitioner who has reached the Stream-entrant's level of practice.

It is simply that desire has lost its authority and the good mind is always in charge. The desires have not gone away completely—they are present, but one is not subject to their controls. A Once-to-be-reborn is someone who has engaged in enough practice that desires have gone away almost completely, such that when a temptation arises outside, the mind experiences one or two desires, but they quickly vanish.

I remember one person who once was a chain smoker and resolved to quit because of poor health, making a tremendous effort in the attempt. Today, about six years later, this person takes great care when with friends who are taking a smoking break at work so as to not succumb to temptation.

If, after spending one's days before practice within the confines of the sentient being and enjoying the pleasures of the five desires, the practitioner encounters the buddhadharma, sets an aspiration, and engages intently in mind-practice, he will encounter the mind of the original nature. As he commits himself sincerely to restoring that mind, he will find himself at war primarily with desires and the notion of self. Through a long period of battling fiercely with the desire and notion of self inside of us, we overcome desires and subdue our self-conceit. But their embers remain in our minds, making their presence known from time to time. We can immediately rid ourselves of such things and send them on their way because we are engaging intently in cultivation of the Way. A Once-to-be-reborn is a bodhisattva for whom such delusions come and go briefly once or twice.

INTERPRETATION

"Subhuti! What do you think? Does the Non-returner have the notion that he has obtained the fruit of the Non-returner?"

"No, World Honored One!" said Subhuti.

"For the Non-returner does not experience any delusions or idle thoughts. Still less does he experience the thought that a delusion has arisen.

Such is the level of practice of the Non-returner."

Nothing But the Mind to Deliver Sentient Beings

The previously mentioned Once-to-be-reborn is one who has performed enough practice that only small embers of desire still remain, so that he experiences a few brief moments of desire when he encounters sensory conditions from outside. The person engaged in Non-returner practice has no desires at all within his mind. No matter what sensory conditions arrive to tempt him from outside, he experiences no desire that arises from the temptation within his mind, and so he can be said to have truly attained no-mind. The person who has performed this much practice is called a "Non-returner," since he has left the worldly realm behind even as he lives in the midst of its sensory conditions of desire.

The Stream-entrant and Once-to-be-reborn described above may lapse through negligence. The Non-returner, in contrast, has built up outstanding abilities and thus will not lapse into the world of sentient beings. This is why he is called a "Non-returner." He is like a rocket that has escaped the Earth's atmosphere.

We have about us what may be called "self-fences." We cannot venture beyond the fence of our home, or the fence of our region, academic ties and religion, or the domains of our race or tribe. The person who has performed practice at the level of the Non-returner, however, can be characterized as a great sage who has broken free completely from his own causes and domains and adopted the entire world as his home, one who sees humankind and all living creatures as his own family and seeks to benefit them.

In *Won*-Buddhism, a person with this level of practice could be described as occupying the status of "beyond the household," for he has fully escaped his own territory. He is a sage who has escaped from all domains of "my group's interests," "my own interests," "my tribe," and so forth, taking the universe for his home and living a life that views all sentient beings as objects of salvation, regardless of whether he possesses affinities with them. Such a person is also called a "heavenly person." The well-known figure of Mahatma Gandhi in India did not live for the people of India alone; he also knew how to feel love for the people of Great Britain, which might be called an enemy nation. Albert Schweitzer, too, sought to save all humankind without confining his efforts to any one people. This is the level attained by a person who is capable of breaking completely free from his own domain to bestow love.

INTERPRETATION

"Subhuti! What do you think? Does the Arhat have the notion of having reaped the fruit of the Arhat?"

"No, World Honored One!" answered Subhuti. "For the name 'Arhat' is given to one who shows not even the slightest notion of belief that he is putting the buddhadharma into practice.

"World Honored One! Were the Arhat to entertain such a thought and say, 'I have achieved the Way of the Arhat,' he would immediately be ensnared by the four misleading concepts.

"World Honored One! You say that I, Subhuti, have achieved samādhi without conflict and become the greatest of practitioners, and you praise me as an Arhat who has left behind all desire for accomplishment, but I do not produce the false notion of being an Arhat who has left desire behind.

"World Honored One! Were I to believe that I have achieved the Way of the Arhat, you would not say that I am enjoying the practice of Aranya.

"But I, Subhuti, truly do live without such a trace.

Thus you bestowed upon me the name of 'one who enjoys the practice of Aranya.'"

The Person Who Delights in No-Mind

If the aforementioned Non-returner is a sage who has reached the level of enjoying tranquility of mind in the no-mind realm and viewing all living creatures as his family, then the Arhat has taken the practice even further, enjoying the no-mind and possessing the ability to produce outstanding achievements through generating a myriad of minds to benefit others.

His mind is peaceful and tranquil at all times and in all places. He is a great bodhisattva and great servant of the world who has left behind all comparing minds, no matter how kind—all minds of distinctions such as distinguishing the good and bad of the world.

It is said even buddhas may have shadows that follow them.

This shadow is the notion: "I have done outstanding work for others. I have examined my mind and found it spotlessly clean. I am the one who has best practiced the Way of Buddhism." Such notions follow them everywhere. The person who has attained the Arhat level of practice is said to be one who has totally broken free of notions, leaving no place for such shadows to set root. He is one fundamentally without any shadow of dispute anywhere in his mind, any question of distinguishing between sides. He is also referred to as the "person of samādhi without conflict."

Generally, people create many barriers. They divide the world into "your religion" and "my religion," "our country" and "other countries," or "our people" and "other people." They fall back on these divisions when formulating their thoughts. In matters of enlightenment and delusion, sacred and profane, they make discriminations, saying, "This is sacred and that is profane."

They think of things as being just or unjust, and they use this as a standard to say that some things are right and others wrong. The person who has reached the Arhat level of practice, however, can be thought of as existing in a state of having escaped completely from such dualistic thoughts of distinction, of sacred and profane, and enjoying the abundance of this one world, becoming a true master of the world with an undivided mind-nature, sensing the pleasure that comes from aiding the world.

The Buddha lived in a quiescent, inactive society, and so, when stating the stages of practice, he focused upon personal practice and composing the mind in terms of study with the precepts, meditation, and wisdom. These are also called the "four stages of Theravāda practice." I believe it would be suited to the practitioner of today if I include here an explanation of a more active approach, one that involves rescuing the world.

> The waters of the Hangang River, a surging sea of water.
> One drop, two drops, how many drops in all?
> Countless droplets come together once and again to flow.
> The brimming smiles of the Arhat.
> Not one moment, not even half of one moment
> simply sending one away.
> He polished the mind, lit the lantern, and delivered gains.
> The thousand days of the sentient being are the Arhat's hour.
> Threaded through with the sincerity of those accumulated minds.
> Ah! Arhat, who has succeeded in the Way!
> Ah! Arhat, who takes pleasure in the Way!

CHAPTER X

PRACTICE TO CULTIVATE THE MIND-FIELD

Cultivation of Splendor on the Pure Land

People race about weeding the fields of others.
Does the Buddha pull the weeds that flourish in his own field?
Stop on your path and turn around. Turn around and return.
When the spring comes, there will be peach blossoms or crabapple flowers,
depending on the time of year.

Said the Buddha to Subhuti, "What do you think? Did the Tathāgata obtain the dharma long ago when he was staying with Dīpaṃkara Buddha?"

"No, World Honored One. When the Tathāgata stayed with Dīpaṃkara Buddha, there is in truth nothing that he obtained in the dharma."

"Subhuti! What do you think? Does the bodhisattva cultivate the splendor of the buddha land?"

"No, World Honored One! For cultivation of the splendor of the buddha land is not cultivation of the splendor, and thus it is called by the name of 'cultivation of the splendor.'"

"Subhuti! Thus all bodhisattvas and mahasattvas should naturally produce a pure mind thus. They should not produce a mind while dwelling on form, they should not produce a mind while dwelling on sound, smell, taste, touch, or ideas, and even when they respond they should produce the mind that is without dwelling.

"Subhuti! If a person's body is likened in its size to King Mt. Sumeru, what you do think? Would you say that such a body is large?"

Said Subhuti, "Very large, World Honored One. For the Buddha has said that the non-body is called by the name of 'large body.'"

This dharma instruction teaches that the splendor of the buddha land is cultivated when the practitioner's mind functions without attachment to anything from outside while encountering and dealing with any sensory condition, whether favorable or adverse. What has adorned our minds? Here, we will learn of the mind that is the most sacred adornment.

Said the Buddha to Subhuti, "Do you believe the Tathāgata obtained the dharma when he was the student of Dīpaṃkara Buddha?"

"No. Even when the Tathāgata cultivated the Way in the order of Dīpaṃkara Buddha, his standard for practice was that realm where nothing is obtained."

Who Was Dīpaṃkara Buddha?

Before Śākyamuni Buddha, six buddhas existed. The last of these was called Dīpaṃkara Buddha. When Śākyamuni Buddha studied, he devoted great belief and sincerity to Dīpaṃkara Buddha. One day, he was walking with Dīpaṃkara Buddha and they came across a place where the ground was muddy, making it difficult to traverse. The story goes that the student Śākyamuni prostrated himself before the feet of Dīpaṃkara Buddha, let down his hair, and thus allowed Dīpaṃkara Buddha to cross over the muddy earth. So total, it is said, was the practitioner Śākyamuni's belief and sincerity toward Dīpaṃkara Buddha, and such was the accumulation of merits with one mind by the monk Śākyamuni, that Dīpaṃkara Buddha prophesied that he one day would undoubtedly become a buddha, the presiding buddha.

From this time, it is said, Śākyamuni Buddha practiced using the unbounded and unchanging original mind realm as his standard. When someone is studying music, he selects a teacher and intently follows along with the teacher's music. If he does so, he will at some point receive the teacher's approval. We may describe the receiving of the teacher's approval as the realm of "musical attainment." In such cases, there is something to be obtained, and a standard exists for determining when someone has not reached a certain level.

But the truth of the mind cannot be expressed in language. It is a realm that has no form and cannot be known, and it is therefore said to be a realm that cannot be defined as any one thing.

It is said that Śākyamuni Buddha saw the nature long ago when he studied with Dīpaṃkara Buddha, and that he used as a standard for practice the mind realm where there is nothing to be obtained. It is impossible to become a sage without practicing based on this standard.

Let us explore the kind of mind that Śākyamuni Buddha attained. In the case of a kind mind, there exists an understanding that allows us to say, "This is a kind mind." Because of this, it is possible to compare one's own kind mind with that of another. The same is true for the loving mind: we say that we love another person so much, and that that person loves us so much. But the mind to which the Buddha awakened cannot be expressed in language, nor can it be estimated in thought. We must seek it out and obtain it.

The mind for which it cannot be said that it exists.

And it cannot be said that it does not exist.

The thing for which it cannot be said that it is black or white,

Or that it is large or small.

The mind that was so yesterday, is so now,

And will be so tomorrow.

That cannot be obtained even if it exists.

And cannot be lost even if it does not exist.

The mind that is so for me, so for you.

And so for the buddha.

Ah—just as it is.

INTERPRETATION

"Subhuti! Do the bodhisattvas think to boast that they have cultivated the splendor of the buddha land?"

"No, World Honored One! For the bodhisattvas' cultivation of the splendor of the buddha land is a true cultivation, one through the mind absent of any boasting mind."

How to Cultivate the Mind-Field

Buddhas and bodhisattvas are people who have cultivated their mind-kingdom, making it wondrous and clean. If you look at the exterior of a temple, a cathedral, or a church, you will find that it has been decorated with inspirational sculptures and wonderful paintings, and that a pure ground of enlightenment has been cultivated, guiding the believer to possess a tranquil and clean mind. Yet buddhas and bodhisattvas, for all their external cultivation of splendor with a clean environment and marvelous facilities, focus their effort first and foremost on their sincere commitment to cultivating the interior of their mind.

Buddhas and bodhisattvas subdue their befouled desires, their minds of hatred and love, their envy, their minds of falsehood, their minds of deception, their laziness and arrogance, and they train their minds, filling them with the mind of faith, the vow to deliver others, the practicing mind, the mind of humility, and the mind of mercy that helps others. Another truly important thing is that all of these different, beautiful minds are the no-mind, the pure mind, and the tranquil mind, unmarked by the taint of any shadow.

What flowers decorate your mind-kingdom? Some of you will have adorned it with love, others with sadness. And there are likely some of you whose mind-kingdom is tainted with pride. Of course, when we are shrouded in worthless minds, we must clear them away and train ourselves with worthy minds of gratitude, of learning, of self-power, and of the spirit of public service. If, despite having trained ourselves with these good minds, we have false ideas and boastful minds, such as the belief that we possess abundant minds of gratitude, this means that our mind is befouled with buds of wickedness sprouting out of a good mind. In every situation, no matter how good our minds may be, we must be grounded in the no-mind and the pure mind.

Thus the first cultivation of splendor by practitioners of the Way in the three periods, the one that they engage in at all times, is none other than the pure mind. It is like washing one's hands before preparing food, a most fundamental cultivation that is required at all times. And upon this clean mind, we must work diligently to instill the mind of mercy, the mind of gratitude, the practicing mind, and so forth.

In a previous chapter, I said that we must produce the mind of charitable giving that has no dwelling. The undwelling mind is a fundamental cultivation of splendor, and we must adorn it with all manner of good and beautiful minds. Depending on the level of our practice, we may cultivate splendor with the clean mind alone, and ignore our cultivation of the minds of charity, gratitude, learning, and so on. Only when we have diligently worked to cultivate all of these can it be said that ours is a consummate and bountiful adornment.

"Subhuti! Thus all bodhisattvas should live with a pure mind free of greed and the four misleading concepts, and should be unbound by sensory conditions such as colors, scents, tastes, tactile sensations, and ideas from the outside. The point is that we must engage in mind-practice whereby all discriminations grounded in the mind are without fixation when encountering any and all sensory conditions."

The Buddhadharma Is Not At All Difficult

People encounter the six types of sensory conditions through the organs that we call the "six roots"—the eye, ear, nose, tongue, body, and mind—and in each case they produce minds of judgment that are put into action. But when ordinary humans and sentient beings encounter favorable or adverse sensory conditions, they form their judgments through the lenses of their own desires and prejudices. The result of this is that they fail to make the right judgments, or they make mistaken judgments, and consequently engage in incorrect actions, becoming shrouded in transgressive karma and experiencing torment.

The Buddha teaches us that when we encounter the six types of sensory conditions we must "empty the mind like the void. Do not fixate anywhere. You must thus possess the no-mind. After you have possessed the void-mind, you must have the right understanding of conditions, make the right judgment for that situation, and put that judgment into action."

When someone with dirty hands prepares a meal, the food will end up being contaminated. Someone who is about to handle food must therefore wash his hands thoroughly first. After that, he must prepare the right ingredients for the meal.

There is a saying in Korean: "Once startled by a tortoise, we are startled by the lid of a pot." Why do we mistake the pot's lid for a tortoise and become startled? It is because the mind that was first startled by the tortoise is still present and colors the mind. Examine your own life closely. Do you find yourself always misunderstanding and distrusting others, being misunderstood and distrusted by them, or maintaining a distance and suffering because of a multitude of desires and prejudices? The buddhadharma is not difficult. It is really very simple. If, when encountering anything, we first make our mind clean, the wisdom to make the right judgment for the conditions will arise. All we have to do then is to put our judgment into practice.

Practice toward emptying the mind, practice toward making right judgments, and practice toward acting upon our judgments represent the heart and foundation of the buddhadharma. This is a very important chapter. This no-mind is called the "mind without dwelling." This is the cultivation of splendor with the pure mind. The production of minds, in turn, leads to the formation of judgments.

It is said that because our judgments determine the course of our life, our profession, and our spouse, we can become someone of outstanding character when we make outstanding judgments. When we make our judgments, however, we do so according to greed and prejudice.

For example, when looking at situations and making judgments, the person from the United States wears American glasses and the person from China wears Chinese glasses. The person we hate is always hateful because we make judgments wearing glasses of hatred, and the one we love always appears lovable because we make judgments wearing glasses of love.

If we avoid becoming attached to desire and bound by prejudice, we will develop the right view, and right decisions will emerge. This means that we should "give rise to the mind"— that is, we must produce the right discriminating minds. The right discriminations will arise when our mind is not obscured by greed or false notions. With all the complex affairs of the world, however, it is not necessarily the case that the right judgment for any given situation will emerge immediately, simply because we have maintained a mind-realm free of discrimination. We must therefore strive constantly to create a realm without dwelling and preserve that mind, and we must also strive ceaselessly to generate the discriminating minds that are proper for the situation.

We need to understand that while instilling the no-mind may be simple—that is to say, the mind with no dwelling—it is extremely difficult to produce the right discriminating minds. When we err in our buddhadharma practice, we speak of the discriminating mind as though it were a hated enemy. Inherently, the possession of no-mind is the fundamental action and goal for producing worthy discriminating minds. All of us must therefore practice toward finding and instilling the undwelling, empty mind free of discriminating minds, and commit ourselves sincerely so that the discriminations that we make for different situations are worthy judgments.

INTERPRETATION

"Subhuti! If a person's body is likened in its size to Mt. Sumeru, do you believe that person is large?"

Said Subhuti, "I would say that he is large, yes, but large within limits. For you have said that only the formless Dharmakāya is truly large without limits."

The Person Who Is Larger than Mt. Sumeru

What kind of person is the great figure, the great person? Whether in the past or in the present, it seems that people who are good-looking and tall in stature have been preferred. We might say that the kings and scholars revered for bequeathing major accomplishments to the world, the people who perform charitable services of welfare for others, are all great people. Consider the fact, however, that the person with a marvelous body is watching that body crumble away at every moment. Beautiful women these days are always showing off their bodies, and it is impossible to understand how someone could be so prideful of this.

People who boast of realizing achievements in the world have reason to do so. Those who rescue people and save societies, those who explore the academic disciplines—these are truly great people. But when they boast of such things, they may become tainted, and they become resentful when others fail to acknowledge them. The person who loves people hates the foe of that people. The person who loves humankind is a truly great person. But let us also consider how we should view animals.

The Buddha said, "The truly great and big person possesses the Dharmakāya Buddha that governs the universe and possesses the Way, holding all humans and living creatures to his bosom and regarding all the world as his home."

At the time, Mt. Sumeru may have been the largest mountain

known. Comparing someone to it may have meant that the person had bequeathed major achievements to society and the country. But the Buddha says that the person with such merits is not a great person. Rather, he says, the truly great person is one who awakens to the truth that governs the universe and puts it into practice. Even a hero who has enjoyed ruling over an age asks the wise sage for instruction and seeks the mind of mercy. Why is the sage capable of moving a hero and turning him into a student? It is because he is possessed of the heavens that rule over all things. There exists a principle that governs all things in the universe without exception. Because of the great power possessed by this principle, it is the very power of heaven and possesses inexhaustible creative transformations. The greatest person is the one possessing this power of heaven.

> The peddler of straw shoes worries when the rain comes.
> The peddler of wooden shoes worries when the clouds clear.
> This worry, that worry, a mountain of worry.
> Within Mt. Sumeru, the dust turns to compost.

CHAPTER XI

THE GREATEST MERIT

The Supremacy of Unconditioned Blessings

Children trade their toys for pieces of gold.

Once grown, the still unwise man sells his mind for treasure.

Ignorant of the path, the practitioner confuses the *mani* pearl with the scriptures.

Past the hill, the road home to the south merely seems distant.

"Subhuti! Were there as many Ganges Rivers as there are grains of sand in the Ganges, what do you think? Would you say the grains of sand in all of those Ganges Rivers are truly numerous?"

Replied Subhuti, "Very numerous, World Honored One! It would be impossible to count all those Ganges Rivers. How much more numerous would be those grains of sand?"

"Subhuti! I am speaking to you now with truthful words. If the virtuous man or the virtuous woman were to perform charitable acts enough to fill as many of the Three Thousand Great Thousand Worlds as there are grains of sand in the Ganges with the seven treasures, would he or she receive many blessings?"

Said Subhuti, "Very many, World Honored One!"

Said the Buddha to Subhuti, "If another virtuous man or virtuous woman accepts the four-line gathas of this sutra and explains them for the sake of others, the blessings and merits would surpass the aforementioned blessings and merits."

Focus on

This dharma instruction teaches that the greatest merit comes from awakening to the self-nature realm taught in the four-line gathas—the core teachings of *The Diamond Sutra*—and to put them into practice, including sharing them with others so that they, too, can practice. In this chapter, we will reflect on what we are currently sharing with others, and to whom. I also hope you will consider why the core doctrine of *The Diamond Sutra* is so important and what it consists of.

"Subhuti! Were there as many Ganges Rivers as there are grains of sand in the Ganges, how many grains of sand would you say there were in all of those rivers?"

Replied Subhuti, "Very many, World Honored One!

Were there as many Ganges Rivers as grains of sand, it would go without saying that there would be more sand in those many Ganges Rivers."

What Kind of Inheritance Are You Preparing?

In his allegories, the Buddha often likened the largest things to Mt. Sumeru and the most numerous things to all the grains of sand in the Ganges.

When the summer comes, I often find myself imagining how many trees there are on Seoul's Mt. Bukhansan, and how many leaves there are on all those trees. Yet all those leaves are fated to fall in the chill autumn wind and float their way down to the ground. Material blessings are ultimately destined to leave us when the time comes.

Someone may work in a field where he performs welfare or charity services for others, providing as many benefits to those worse off as there are trees in nature. But even these efforts are limited and destined to finally scatter away when the time comes. Not only are the benefits that we give others through material things finite, but the spirit may actually be ravaged by that material abundance, and we will be unable to offer the ultimate in human happiness.

What are you planning to leave as an inheritance to your offspring? Your child may be pleased to inherit great material wealth. But have you ever worried that his humanity might be damaged by the riches, that he will become lazy and live a misguided life with skewed values? I saw many wealthy people ruined by the national trauma of Korea's foreign exchange crisis. These people suffered from their ruination, blaming society and wandering in a morass of falsehoods, transgressions, and evil that can never be undone.

The Buddha earnestly counsels us that neither we nor others can attain true peace of mind when our life is oriented toward the material.

While it is important to leave our children a material legacy, my hope is that we will become the wonderful parents who are capable of leaving a legacy of instilling virtuous habits, a legacy of faith in the buddhadharma, a legacy of practice of the buddhadharma, and a legacy of the true mind that is the no-mind realm.

"Subhuti! I am speaking the truth to you now.

If the virtuous man or the virtuous woman were to perform enough charitable services to fill the Three Thousand Great Thousand Worlds with the seven treasures, how great in number would be the merits that return as recompense?"

Said Subhuti, "Very great, World Honored One!"

Said the Buddha to Subhuti,

"If another virtuous man or virtuous woman properly practices the four-line gathas that are the core of *The Diamond Sutra* and explains them for the sake of others, the merits would be far greater still."

The Mind of Incalculable Value

The Buddha often stresses that his words contain no falsehood. Try to imagine why this might be. I believe that he said this from time to time when the audience did not comprehend his meaning clearly, or when the truths that he taught seemed very divorced from their reality. All of you reading these words right now may find it staggering to imagine all the merits that would return to someone who practiced charitable services to others with as many treasures as there are grains of sand in the Ganges River. You may not comprehend the Buddha when he says that this is less than what one receives for putting the four-line gathas into practice and communicating them to others. It shows a mature understanding of the buddhadharma and the higher-level life, however, when we awaken to the fact that these words are a sure truth.

When we pursue material abundance alone, we become slaves to material things. Those who campaign for some outstanding belief system live at the beck and call of love and hatred, viciously criticizing opposing groups and boasting of the excellence of their own ideas. Those who view the good mind as most important are governed by a sense of pride in having done good things. Those who pursue beauty alone cannot be free from the mind that objectifies things as beautiful or ugly. Let us examine, then, what the Buddha is telling us to do.

The four-line gatha is an expression of the core teachings of *The Diamond Sutra* in verse form. These gathas teach us of the true suchness mind and tathāgata mind existing within our mind. I explained in a previous chapter about how this is the dharma of no-action. As the first stage toward understanding the content of the gathas, we must believe that a buddha mind exists in our mind, and second, we must search for and awaken to that mind. At the next stage, we must preserve that mind at all times and places without losing it. This is followed by a stage of cultivating blessings and happiness by using that mind appropriately whenever we have affairs to attend to.

When we have performed this mind-practice with certainty, we will gain the ability to enjoy peace in our mind at all times, leaving behind questions of the good or bad of our environment, the presence and absence of money, our possession or lack of privileges and knowledge. Furthermore, we will gain the ability to control money and to become active agents in making use of honors and privileges, knowledge, truth, good, and beauty. And we will gain the miraculous ability to control all things in the universe as we wish.

The person who designs machinery is called an engineer. The person who directs others is called a leader, and the person who has trained his mind well is called a practitioner of the Way or a sage. Both the engineer and the leader are subject to the controls of the mind. It could therefore be said that mind-practice is the foundation of all skills.

What the Buddha is saying here is that when we engage in mind-practice ourselves, and encourage others to do the same, we will be able to succeed with the material and technical things outside, and that studying the four-line gathas and teaching them to others constitutes the greatest of all merits.

The life of the ordinary human, caught in the bear's paw.

Through the generations, a bear's paw is passed down.

One after another, they are drawn and drawn again

to cycle through the destinies.

What do the buddhas pass down?

This is transmission merely in secrets.

They pass down only a dharma of grasping and releasing.

CHAPTER XII

THE PLACE WHERE THE DIAMOND SUTRA IS PRESENT

Revering the Proper Teaching

Oh, begging traveler laden with gold,
In his mercy, Bhisma Garjitasvara Raja gave the diamond mirror.
Do not be deceived by the face reflected in the mirror,
The formless face, the nameless face.
Only the self-nature light shines in that face.

"Furthermore, Subhuti! When you teach others about this sutra, or even only its four-line gathas, you should understand this. The place where you do so will be venerated by all heavenly beings and asuras in all realms as a stupa and shrine to the Buddha. This is to say nothing of he who accepts and upholds, reads and recites it in its entirety.

Subhuti! You should understand this. Such a person will achieve the supreme and rarest dharma.

In the place where this scripture is found, it is as though one is in the presence of the Buddha and his venerable disciples."

Focus on

Here, the Buddha explains about the importance of *The Diamond Sutra* and the great merits of practicing its Way and principle. It is not merely humans that dwell in this world. There are worlds of denizens of hell, sentient beings, animals, and hungry ghosts without bodies, and there is a higher world of gods. These spiritual beings and hungry ghosts also wish to progress, however, and so they seek to understand the buddhadharma of the Buddha and to guard and honor the place occupied by *The Diamond Sutra* in which the essence of the buddhadharma is contained. In this chapter, we will learn about the worlds of the six destinies and the importance of *The Diamond Sutra*.

"I tell you this once again, Subhuti! When you teach others about this sutra and the four-line gathas as you met with your affinities, the place where you do so will be the site of offerings given by all human beings, heavenly beings, and asuras as though it were a stupa and shrine to the Buddha. And this is to say nothing of the merits that come to him who practices the Way and principle of *The Diamond Sutra* perfectly."

Grasp the Core of the Buddhadharma

In the past, the lack of printing technology meant that people who wished to read the scriptures had to transcribe them with a particular power of aspiration. Furthermore, because so few people sought to read *The Diamond Sutra*, it was seen only by special people who wrote it out by hand and came to possess it in that way. It was also explained only to those with exceptionally high spiritual capacity, since its contents could not be understood by all people. For this reason, the Buddha said that the place where *The Diamond Sutra* is present is the enlightenment ground of a buddha, as it is home to great students and people practicing the teachings of the sutra. These days, however, any student of Buddhism is likely to have a copy of *The Diamond Sutra* at home. As such, where there is someone who works intently to read and practice the sutra and to explain it to others, that place is none other than the enlightenment ground of a buddha. In particular, it is enough to consider that *The Diamond Sutra* lies in the place where we have enshrined the one circle image of the Il-Won-Sang.

In the very last chapter, there is an explanation of the *Diamond Sutra* Way and principle of the one unity image—the truth that all things are one. The one unity image and the Il-Won-Sang refer to the same thing. The home where the Il-Won-Sang is enshrined is the enlightenment ground of a buddha, and the place occupied by the person who keeps the Il-Won-Sang in mind always, admiring it and putting it into practice even in his sleep and dreams, is none other than a buddha place and the enlightenment ground of a buddha. The "four-line gatha" here suggests the core and specific object of the truth.

There was a monk named Shitou Xiqian, who had a student named Xianshi. The two of them were walking along when they found their way blocked by a tree branch.

Shitou Xiqian turned to Xianshi and said, "Cut down that tree."

"Give me an axe," replied Xianshi.

Shitou Xiqian took an axe and removed the blade. "Here," he said, handing the blade to Xianshi.

"Why are you only giving me the blade?" asked Xianshi. "Why don't you give me the handle?"

"What need have you for a handle?" answered Shitou Xiqian. "If you want to cut down a tree, you need the blade of the axe."

At that moment, it is said, Xianshi experienced awakening.

What is it that the four-line gathas of *The Diamond Sutra* are trying to give us? We need to strip away all the excess and grab hold of the core.

What is the core of the buddhadharma? What kind of minds are exchanged among buddhas? As you read these lectures, you need to understand the axe with no handle, and you need to be able to play a tune on a flute with no holes. If you find this impossible, you will wander the darkness for thousands of years in endless misfortune, and if you find it easy you will merely craft a light transmission verse and go through the motions of being an enlightened master— an even more undesirable outcome. What kind of place is the realm that is neither simple nor difficult?

In a capitalist society, there is almost nothing that you cannot do if you have money. People are even released from prison on bail after committing crimes. The absolute might of money is something truly formidable.

In Buddhism, it is believed that if we simply understand the realm that the four-line gathas teach, we can attain buddhahood, and we will encounter no problems on our road to the next life, we will break free from a hell of torment and hatred, and we will also escape the power of karmic action that has accumulated over countless eons. It is a truly tremendous jewel, one that lets us avoid being befouled even when we spend and spend money, and become arrogant when we have power in our grasp. So important is this realm, it may be said, that the place occupied by such a person (the place of the person who explains *The Diamond Sutra*) is learned of first by the heavenly beings and asuras, who hover around such a person to receive the dharma and leave offerings.

If you go to a temple, you will find the Four Devas. It is said that when a person of great faith visits the temple, the Four Devas go first to greet him as a precious guest. Among the ghosts, there are also said to be good spirits that love the buddhadharma. They gather in the places where the greatest scriptures—those of *The Diamond Sutra*—are taught. They rejoice in hearing the scriptures and leave offerings—merits that result in progression. When we understand the core of *The Diamond Sutra* and put it into practice, all the people around us will respect us, and the heavenly beings and asuras will offer their unseen protection, opening the road before us and guiding us forward.

"Subhuti! The person who awakens to the meaning of *The Diamond Sutra* and puts it into practice is one who has practiced the most worthy dharma in the eternal world. It may therefore be said that wherever those scriptures are found, it is as though one is in the presence of a buddha or his venerable students."

Sacred Values Are the Highest Values

In this world, the standards for our values are categorized into truth, goodness, and beauty. These are also described as universal human values, since they remain unchanged in every world. They include the truths discovered through deep devotion to research in the ivory tower of academia; the works of charity and welfare through which we offer good to all those in need; and the beautiful creations of innumerable artists. Yet there is a supreme value that transcends all of these worthy things. This is called the "sacred value."

For example, people often use the word *sacred* to describe Beethoven, someone who composed beautiful music. All classes of people esteem the holy sages of humankind. Regardless of differences of race, ideas, ethnicity, or era, we have the mind to respect and love all sages, for this is the supreme value. *The Diamond Sutra* spoken of here does not tell the people studying and mastering it to realize values of truth, goodness, and beauty, but to germinate the seeds of a sage.

What is described here, then, is the rarest of human beings. Only when we intently study the meaning of *The Diamond Sutra* and form the sacred character that is most worthy will we find a way to repay our debt of gratitude to the Buddha for speaking the words of this sutra for us.

Dinstinctions of worth and worthlessness, more or less.

Right and wrong—the scattered lives of snowflakes.

Ten million phantom flowers from a single speck in the eye.

For the tathāgata said that the greatest value is the no-value.

CHAPTER XIII

DECIDING THE TITLE OF THE SCRIPTURE

Accepting and Upholding in Accordance with the Dharma

My master is gone, but remains whole in my mind.

What point is there in drawing a picture?

Not and nothing, this is the noble "alone honored" tradition

of only his royal family.

Who will exist to recognize this tradition outside of traditions?

At this time, Subhuti said to the Buddha, "World Honored One! What is the name of this sutra, and how should we accept and respectfully uphold it?"

Said the Buddha to Subhuti, "The name of this instruction is the *Vajracchedika-Prajñāpāramitā*. Revere it and uphold it under that name. For Subhuti! The '*Prajñāpāramitā*' spoken by the Buddha is not the *Prajñāpāramitā*, and thus it is called by the name of '*Prajñāpāramitā*.'

Subhuti! What do you think? Does there exist a teaching of the dharma by the Tathāgata?"

Said Subhuti to the Buddha, "World Honored One! There is no dharma that the Tathāgata has taught."

"Subhuti! What do you think? Would you say that there are many specks of dust in the Three Thousand Great Thousand Worlds?"

Said Subhuti, "Very many, World Honored One."

"Subhuti! The Tathāgata says that none of these specks of dust are specks of dust, and so they are called by the name of 'specks of dust.' Likewise, the 'worlds' spoken of by the Tathāgata are not worlds, and thus are called by the name of 'worlds.'

Subhuti! What do you think? Can one recognize the Tathāgata from the thirty-two marks?"

"No, World Honored One! One cannot recognize the Tathāgata from the thirty-two marks. For the 'thirty-two marks' spoken of by the Tathāgata are not those marks, and thus are called by the name of 'thirty-two marks.'"

"Subhuti! Even if a virtuous man or virtuous woman devotes as many lifetimes as there are grains of sand in the Ganges to performing charitable service, if another person accepts and upholds even the four-line gathas of this sutra and explains them to others, the blessings will be far greater."

Focus on

We must understand the meaning of the title of this sutra, the *Vajracchedika-Prajñāpāramitā-Sūtra*, and study the true meaning of affirmation and negation. We will also study how those who have seen the outstanding physical qualities of the buddha's thirty-two marks must not confuse this beauty with the buddha's character.

At this time, Subhuti said to the Buddha,

"World Honored One! What is the name of the dharma instruction that you have given, and how should we honor it?"

Said the Buddha to Subhuti, "The name of this instruction is the *Vajracchedika-Prajñāpāramitā*. Revere it and practice it under that name. But Subhuti! The *Prajñāpāramitā* of which I have just spoken is merely a name, and not the true reality of the *Prajñāpāramitā*."

What Do *Vajracchedika, Prajñā,* and *Pāramitā* Mean?

I explained above about the meaning of the name *Vajracchedika-Prajñāpāramitā*. *Vajracchedika*, or "diamond," describes the realm of self-nature, the foundation nature of the mind. *Prajñā* refers to a light that surges forth from the self-nature, while *pāramitā*, a word that means "to cross," signifies practice. We use the term *pāramitā* to describe our practice toward ridding ourselves of defilements and idle thoughts and restoring our self-nature. It is a process of ridding ourselves of the torments of defilement, creating the ultimate bliss of the self-nature, moving our one mind from discord to harmony, and practicing to reach the buddha ground.

The universe may be large in mass, but there are three principles that determine its operation. First, we can observe the workings of creative transformation. For example, we can witness the changing seasons and the coming of spring, summer, and autumn. The thing that makes this so is called "creative transformation." But what exists such that the correct creative transformations take place? The answer is wisdom and light. This we call *prajñā*, or "the light of truth." It is also described with the term *won-gwang*, or "the (perfect) circle light," meaning the light that penetrates through all things.

Where does this *prajñā* light come from? It comes from a foundation that is utterly empty. Such is the case with our mind. The empty mind is the realm of self-nature—this is indicated with the word "diamond." Many different thoughts emerge from the empty diamond realm. This is our light, and the realm of the all-penetrating circle. When we take our thought and put it into practice, this is called "rightness" and "creative transformation." At first, there is the foundation of the diamond self-nature. Next, there is the *prajñā* or light, and after that there is the creative transformation of practice. This is also the sequence followed by the Dharmakāya truth that governs the universe.

The Threefold Study—Cultivation, Inquiry, and Choice in Action—is, ultimately, practice toward making the three elements of Dharmakāya Buddha operation, or Il-Won-Sang operation, our own through training of the human character. Cultivating the Spirit refers to our entering the diamond self-nature realm of truth. This is also called the absorption realm. Inquiry into Human Affairs and Universal Principles refers to our efforts to understand all things according to the light within. This is also known as the wisdom realm. Choice in Action refers to our putting into practice what we have understood through the light. This is the realm of precepts. This Threefold Study of absorption, wisdom, and precepts emerges from the idea that we should behave just as the truth does. We are not being told to practice and perform the Threefold Study without any basis in truth.

Understand the Original Intent of the Buddha's Teachings

In this chapter, we find a passage that is very difficult to interpret. "Subhuti!" the Buddha says. "The *Prajñāpāramitā* of which I have just spoken is merely a name, and not the true image of the *Prajñāpāramitā*." I will explain this by way of example. Consider a set of meditation beads. It is a good tool for helping us with our practice. So when we are told to practice with meditation beads, there is a difference between the beads themselves and the words "meditation beads." The cake described in words and the real cake are two different things.

Likewise, *The Diamond Sutra* is a picture book about the mind. The thing called the *Vajracchedika-Prajñāpāramitā* is a scripture, not the diamond wisdom and practice inside of us. The scripture is not something within us, but merely a name that denotes it. To elaborate, the Buddha is saying, "Do not allow yourself to be bound by the letter. The original intent of my teaching is that you should get hold of your mind, discover it, and practice by way of the letter."

In the Buddha's day, there were many teachers of treatises, and logical analyses of language flourished.

Whether they came from scriptures or the spoken language, names were widely discussed in Indian society, and I imagine that these words were most likely raised quite frequently.

To elaborate, the Buddha is communicating an earnest message saying, "The reason I am speaking now of '*The Diamond Sutra*' is to teach about the mind. While you should adopt it as a standard for mind-practice and take it as your mind mirror, I implore you not to fixate on the language and the letter in studying *The Diamond Sutra*."

When you look into a mirror, you will see your own face. No one sees the face reflected back at him and fails to understand that it is not the real self. But ordinary humans do confuse the self reflected in the mirror with the real self. The person who sees someone dirty in the mirror should wash himself; only a fool would try to clean the mirror. The Buddha is earnestly entreating us to find our image in the mirror of *The Diamond Sutra*. Why question the image that appears in this mirror? *The Diamond Sutra* is merely a mirror that accurately reflects us. But that name, *The Diamond Sutra*, is merely the title of a scripture—a finger pointing to the moon.

Previously, the Buddha said that this was akin to a raft that you must abandon once you have crossed to the other side. To explain it one more time in a bit more detail, let me use the example of a recording device. We have a word that refers to that device, and we have our concept of the recorder. At times, we fail to see properly— we confuse and mistake the word "recorder," the real recorder, and the concept of a recorder. We may have the idea that foreign-made recorders are better, so that imported products look better to us even when the quality of domestic recorders has improved. In this way, we are told to focus mainly on breaking free from the concepts within and the ideas expressed in words, and on finding the true image.

INTERPRETATION

"Subhuti! Do you believe it possible for the Tathāgata to express in words the dharma that is the true image?" Said Subhuti, "I do not think it is possible to preach the dharma wholly in words."

Speak the Mind That Cannot Be Spoken

No matter how pure they may be, the material things and ideas in this world are all mixtures of various elements. Nothing continues maintaining the same form through changes in place and time. Even when we describe these real entities effectively in speech and writing, our narrative is doomed to inadequacy. Moreover, these things may be depicted in very different ways depending on the perspective of the narrator.

When we look at paintings, we can see that different painters render the same object in different shapes and colors depending on their own aesthetic sense. But the truth that is a reality neither seen, nor heard, nor grasped, and the Way that we keep with us in our mind, can never be perfectly explained—even by a buddha. Because the Way and principle of that reality is a realm that can never be understood through words and discriminating minds, you must understand that the Buddha was compelled in this section to express the realm of the diamond self-nature verbally for the purposes of teaching that it is a realm that cannot be expressed in words, a realm that cannot be called by name.

The poor, poor buddha,
When he puts it into words, he forsakes the diamond.
And if there are no words he defies mercy. Oh dear, oh dear.
To say that one has not spoken even after speaking.
Go ask the Maitreya who merely smiles.

"Subhuti! What do you think? The Tathāgata cannot fully explain the nature of the truth realm that exists even in the smallest speck among the myriad phenomena of the universe, or the truth realm that is immanent in the entire world. For both the speck and the world are merely names and not their specific objects."

See the Buddha in a Speck of Dust

Innumerable material things exist within this universe. The number of things that make up our universe may truly be without limit. The term *speck* here describes the limitlessness of the objects that surround us, while the term *world* is similar to what we often speak of in referring to similar things in groups, as in the "world of insects," "world of beasts," "world of sentient beings," or "world of buddhas."

All around the everyday lives of us humans are objects, and the worlds that represent their combination. The result is that we are forever maintaining relationships of negotiation. We constantly view these material things and worlds through the lens of prejudice, without seeing them as they truly are. And we form judgments based on these prejudices, spending our lives amid thoughts of the "good" and "bad" of things.

There exists a sacred world and a profane world, as commonly conceived by humankind. There is also a system of dualistic thinking with a world of truth and a world of phenomena. This is a deeply misguided system of thought. The world of truth and the sacred world do not exist separately, and the material things that we call "tainted" may at times serve as convenient tools that enrich our lives.

These concepts of "good" or "bad," "worthy" or "worthless," "virtuous" or "evil," and so forth are simply names that we assign on a given occasion for the sake of convenience. If we see rightly without being deceived by names, we will understand that the specks of the myriad phenomena of the universe and the different worlds into which they are grouped are entirely and equally masses of truth bearing the diamond self-nature, and that there lies concealed within them a Way and principle that can punish us or grant us blessings.

All things in this world harbor a principle within them. There exists no world that is not governed by the dharma of principle. For this reason, all are realms of buddha nature, and even the tiniest specks are buddha images and tathāgatas.

"Subhuti! Can one simply declare the Tathāgata a buddha after seeing the thirty-two marks of his wondrous aspect?"

Replied Subhuti, "No, World Honored One!

One cannot say that someone is a Tathāgata from his aspect, for the thirty-two marks of which you spoke are not the truth. They are called by the name of the 'thirty-two marks of the Tathāgata.'"

Believe Not in the Person Alone, but See the Dharmakāya

We deluded sentient beings often make predeterminations about the content of something based merely on its exterior. Of course, there are instances in which the exterior and substance match. But we also find many cases where the substance of an object does not necessarily match its exterior. In addition, sentient beings carry with them all manner of prejudices. When we hold prejudices, useful things may become useless and useless things useful, depending on our values.

The Buddha possessed a truly marvelous face and body. These were the result of his creation of blessings and his outstanding management of his mind. When someone creates blessings through this sort of mind management, we call it "character." This physical beauty and this character are phenomena. Whether something is an external phenomenon or an internal phenomenon, it is a phenomenon nonetheless. But there exists a truth, the true manifestation of the Dharmakāya, that makes the character and body so.

At the heart of the Buddha's question here is the concern that most of the Buddhists who believe in and follow him are merely doing so because they admire and revere the buddha phenomenon of his outstanding physical beauty, and that they have no interest in the tathāgata realm, the unchanging mind realm, that exists within him and all people. He repeatedly urges them to awaken to the Dharmakāya Buddha within him and themselves, rather than simply admiring his embodiment.

He is saying that while they may have felt admiration upon seeing the buddha's embodiment—his physical beauty—they did not locate the Dharmakāya teacher within themselves—the Way and principle—and that they must awaken to this. Ordinary sentient beings express their admiration after merely seeing the lushness of the fruit and leaves on the tree. The wise person considers the profusion of roots that enabled those fruits and leaves to be. When we are looking at the buddha or at any of the objects in this universe, we must have the discernment to see the news of the dharma-realm within phenomena that enables those phenomena to be, and to apply this in actual practice.

INTERPRETATION

"Subhuti! Even if a virtuous man or virtuous woman devotes as many lifetimes as there are grains of sand in the Ganges to performing charitable service, the blessings and merits will be far greater for another person who awakens to the principle of this scripture, practices it, and communicates it to others."

The Difference Between Sacred Karma and Good Karma

All living creatures with a soul have experienced not only this life, but innumerably many previous ones, and they will continue to enjoy eternal life in the days to come. Those who do not understand will say that someone has died. The buddha or bodhisattva, however, will say that it is merely the body that has died, and that the soul has not. The soul, he will say, goes and then comes again. This is so. Dying means that our body is spent and we can no longer use it. It does not mean that our soul is gone.

The Buddha says that a person may perform charitable acts for others for as many lifetimes as there are grains of sand in the Ganges—in today's terms, this may be described as innumerable acts of welfare—but while he will receive boundless blessings as a result, such a person is not a buddha or bodhisattva who is also skilled at use of the mind. In other words, the Buddha is expressing that such charity is, as merits go, far lower than that of teaching the way of practice toward proper use of the mind.

Mining gold and giving it to someone else cannot be compared to mining and giving coal. The praise that a person receives for doing good works and the respect that a person earns for teaching sacred values exist at fundamentally different levels.

Two people may engage in the same amount of effort for the same length of time, but when they engage in efforts for the sacred, they produce what is called "sacred karma," and when they engage in efforts for the good, they produce "good karma." With good karma, it is possible that they will cycle through destinies and experience torment, but the sacred karma from sharing the sacred mind-practice and dharma of the buddha is different in that it allows us free command of our destiny.

CHAPTER XIV

TRUE PRACTICE WITH FORBEARANCE

Leaving Notions and Achieving Cessation

The sky is empty, the earth silent,
The mountains are blue and the waters flow.
How faint, the prince's news.
The green grass sprouts in patches on the hill in spring.
How many springs has it seen, that seldom visited hill?

At this time, Subhuti, upon hearing the teaching of this sutra, understood its meaning profoundly, shedding tears and weeping sadly.

"Rare World Honored One!" he said to the Buddha. "Never before have I heard with the wisdom eye that I obtained from long ago a sutra with as profound a meaning as that which the Buddha has just spoken.

World Honored One! Should another person find and hear this sutra and have a pure mind of belief, he will immediately produce a true notion, and such a person will be able to accomplish the rarest of merits.

World Honored One! This true notion is not this notion, and thus the Tathāgata refers to it by the name of 'true notion.'

World Honored One! It is not difficult for me to hear the scripture now, to believe it, understand it, and accept it and uphold it. But the sentient being who, in the last five hundred years in the coming world, hears this sutra and believes it, understands it, accepts it and upholds it will be the rarest of all. For such a person will have not harbor conceptions of the self, the person, the sentient being, or long life.

Why is this so? The conception of the self will not be the conception of the self, and the conceptions of the person, the sentient being, and long life will not be those conceptions.

For the name of 'buddha' is given when one is separated from all notions."

"Yes," said the Buddha to Subhuti. "It is just so.

If there is someone who hears this sutra and experiences neither astonishment nor fear, then you should understand this. Such a person will be a true rarity.

For Subhuti! The greatest pāramitā of which the Tathāgata spoke is not the greatest pāramitā, and thus it is called by the name of 'greatest pāramitā.'

Subhuti! The Tathāgata teaches that the pāramitā of forbearance is not the pāramitā of forbearance, and thus it is called by the name of 'pāramitā of forbearance.'

For Subhuti! When I long ago had my body dismembered by the King of Kalinga, I had no conception of the self, the person, the sentient being, or long life.

For if I had had conceptions of the self, the person, the sentient being, or long life long ago while my body was being cut to pieces, I would have produced minds of anger and resentment.

Subhuti! I also recall that I was devoid of conceptions of the self, the person, the sentient being, and long life in the worlds when I cultivated the Way five hundred lifetimes ago as a hermit practitioner of ascetism.

Thus Subhuti! The bodhisattvas should leave behind all notions and set the aspiration of achieving the Anuttara-Samyak-Sambodhi mind.

He should not produce minds dwelling on form, he should not produce minds dwelling on sound, smell, taste, touch, or ideas, and he should produce the mind without dwelling.

If there is dwelling of the mind, then this is not true dwelling. For this reason, the Buddha said, "The bodhisattva does not perform charitable acts while abiding with his mind on form."

Subhuti! The bodhisattva must perform acts of generosity so that all sentient beings benefit in this way. Thus none of the forms of which the Tathāgata spoke is a form, nor are all the sentient beings spoken of sentient beings.

Subhuti! The Tathāgata speaks words that are true, speaks words that are sincere, and speaks words that are unchanging. He speaks words that are not deceptive, and he speaks words that do not differ.

Subhuti! The dharma obtained by the Tathāgata is neither substantial nor insubstantial.

Subhuti! When the bodhisattva performs acts of charity while dwelling with the mind on a dharma, he is similar to a person who has entered the darkness and cannot see. And when he performs acts of charity without dwelling with the mind on the dharma, it is as though his eye can distinguish all the different colors reflected in the bright rays of the sun.

Subhuti! If the virtuous man and woman of the coming world are capable of accepting and upholding, reading and reciting this sutra, the Tathāgata will know all and see all about this person with the buddha's wisdom, and they will achieve attainment of all these limitless and boundless merits."

Focus on

In this section, Subhuti recapitulates the dharma instruction on *The Diamond Sutra*, reiterating and emphasizing what has been said up to this point and receiving authentication from the Buddha. In this chapter, we will need to examine how the emergence of a new form of buddhadharma was prophesied for the world of the declining dharma, as well as summarize the reader's impressions upon reading *The Diamond Sutra*. We will also study the forbearance *pāramitā* and why fixation on it is a problem.

At this time, Subhuti, having listened respectfully to the Buddha's dharma instruction on *The Diamond Sutra*, awakened deeply to the truth and experienced profound emotion.

"Oh rare World Honored One!" he said.

"Never before have I encountered with my wisdom eye scriptures with as profound a meaning as those that you have just spoken."

What Are You Searching For Right Now?

A figure of supreme wisdom, Subhuti expresses his respect for the Buddha's detailed instruction thus far on the diamond self-nature, *prajñā* wisdom, and the practice toward reaching the hill of the buddha. He ultimately finds himself weeping tears of overwhelming emotion.

Subhuti is tremendously gratified to have received instruction on what he had been seeking. His tears come because he shares the same feelings as the buddha, who has spoken everything inside of Subhuti at a moment when Subhuti was gaining awakening to the *Diamond Sutra* truth, and on the verge of achieving enlightenment.

The reader, too, may shed tears here. We must be seekers of the Way. The person who seeks the Way will be so grateful as to be moved to tears upon reading the scriptures and encountering the words of a sage, while other people may not experience any particular emotional response.

When one has searched and searched for the Way, he is grateful to receive instruction on the Way, he is even happier to awaken to it, and he is more profoundly moved still when he hears that dharma instruction as he puts it into practice himself.

What is it that you are earnestly searching for at this moment? Is it something worthy and eternal? Or is it something temporary? Are you searching for something that has to do with physical desires or the worldly? It is said that if people put even half the effort into seeking the Way and the buddhadharma that they put into the worldly things that they seek, then there is no Way that could not be attained. We do not need to view it as something out of reach. If we simply understand what it is that we are seeking and change course toward working for it, pleasure will immediately come of this, and further efforts will bring us the experience of the surging joy of dharma.

When a hen lays an egg, she devotedly sits atop the egg from which her chick will emerge. About three weeks later, it is said, the chick knocks on the inside of the egg as if to say to its mother, "I'm ready to come out now." The hen hears this and pecks at the shell from outside, whereupon the chick inside is able to break the egg open and come out. When the seeker of the Way accumulates merits with utmost sincerity and directs his gaze toward a teacher upon receiving great news, the teacher recognizes this and offers authentication. How great this pleasure is when a student receives authentication!

INTERPRETATION

"World Honored One! Should another person hear this sutra and produce a pure belief, he will immediately realize the true notion, and such a person will unquestionably accomplish a rare merit.

"But World Honored One! This true notion has no form of any kind. For this reason, the Tathāgata has referred to it by the name of 'true notion.'"

Self-Power and Other-Power Minds of Faith

In truth, the reason that we want to hear the dharma instruction of *The Diamond Sutra*, to assess it against our minds, and to awaken to it is because we have heard the dharma instructions of the Buddha over the course of many lifetimes, or we have been influenced by the Buddha's marvelous character by way of his students and come to believe in the buddhadharma in that way, working hard to live according to his teachings and put them into practice. All of you reading about *The Diamond Sutra* now had minds of faith and practice in previous lives. I urge you to listen with a sense of pride in this fact.

As a young man, Huineng, the sixth patriarch of China's Sŏn masters, lost his father at an early age and had to care for his widowed mother. He sold timber and used the money from it to support her. One day, he was selling timber at the market and a customer asked him to deliver an order to his house. Huineng carried the timber all the way over to the house.

In today's terms, we would call it an inn. One of the guests there was reading aloud from *The Diamond Sutra*. Huineng heard the guest reciting the passage about "giving rise to a mind that, even while responding, does not abide anywhere" and awakened instantly to its meaning. He asked the name of the scripture and where he might go to study it. He heard that it was called *The Diamond Sutra* and that he could study it with the teacher Daman Hongren, the fifth patriarch. It was through joining the order immediately and studying intently that he came to be a great teacher himself, someone who might be called the father of the revival of Chinese Buddhism. Some people are like this, and experience a dramatic awakening of the mind after hearing just a word of the dharma instruction, while others experience a maturing of their practice over time. What is clear, however, is that both of these awakenings depend upon the earnest vow to seek the buddhadharma, and the sincere commitment to put this into practice.

Generally, people begin without knowledge of the realm of truth. They learn of it later through a dharma instruction and come to harbor questions, experiencing awakening and putting it into practice. The awakened person hears a dharma instruction and thinks, "Ah, yes! That person is explaining what I have come to know," and thus comes to go through the procedure of authentication. Such an experience of sure awakening could be called the "self-power mind of faith." Other people, in contrast, hear a dharma instruction and produce the mind of faith, saying, "Ah, so it is," before they achieve awakening. When it is produced without awakening, it could be called the "other-power mind of faith." The deeper this other-power mind of faith is, the faster the mind of faith in awakening may appear. Furthermore, the practice and realization of this mind realm in one's daily life with a mind of firm faith through one's own efforts represent a higher state of conviction.

"World Honored One! It is not difficult for me to listen respectfully to the *Diamond Sutra* dharma instruction now, to believe it, understand it, and put it into practice. But the person who, among sentient beings more than 2,500 years hence, hears this scripture and believes it, understands it, and puts it into practice will be a very rare person indeed. For such a person will have engaged in practice devoid of the four misleading concepts. Such a person unbound by the four misleading concepts has a self but is not bound by images. He will distinguish people, long life, and sentient beings at will, and engage in the life of the middle way without being bound to images. It will be possible to call him a buddha who has left behind all notions, including notions of existence and non-existence."

"Yes," said the Buddha to Subhuti. "It is just so."

Subhuti's Worries About the Age of Declining Dharma

Subhuti, a student of the Buddha, appears to have possessed a tremendous spiritual sense. While everyone happily produced minds of faith upon hearing the dharma instruction, he was moved to tears of powerful emotion. Moreover, even though the Buddha was present there at that moment, he asked his question out of concern for what would become of people after the Buddha's nirvana. I believe that this may have been because Subhuti was someone who often experienced profound concerns about human minds in the world of the declining dharma age.

The person without wisdom thinks only of the immediate reality. The wise person considers and prepares for the future. Subhuti, however, appears to have been an exceptional individual, as his concerns extended to a time several millennia hence.

Judging from the current state of human understanding, the reference to the last 500 years after the Buddha's nirvana appears to have provided a fairly good indication of the current age of declining dharma—an age of world-ending crisis. The Buddha says in this chapter that among those of you encountering *The Diamond Sutra* now, there is unquestionably someone who produces the mind of faith, saying, "Ah, so this is how it will be," who awakens to the mind realm, thinking, "Ah, so it is," and who possesses the mind of realization, saying, "I, too, have done so in the past."

If, upon looking around you, you encounter someone who is like this, someone you recognize as having practiced over the course of countless past lives, I hope that you will examine how far along you are yourself.

When we first begin cultivating the Way, we are constantly

being tormented by desires. But once those desires have been conquered, the practitioner is tormented by the notion of "myself," discriminating minds of "you," and feelings of inferiority and superiority that follow him around like shadows. A notion is like a blindfold or a mist that prevents us from seeing in front and back of ourselves. When a practitioner is intoxicated with notions, he may not commit grave transgressions and evil, but the notions prevent him from ever being free. They obscure his wisdom, block him from further advancement, and hinder minds of mercy. This is unquestionably something that the bodhisattva must overcome.

If there is one phrase that could be said to represent the entirety of the *The Diamond Sutra* lesson, I believe it is the instruction to rid ourselves of notions. We must understand the meaning of the buddha's earnest exhortation and become great enlightened ones who are free of notions.

The wicked person and kind person alike live in shadow.
A phantom that follows the pure person, and the bodhisattva as well.
The mind of effort turns into a thief.
When he ceases his efforts and realizes the no-mind in coming and going.
He will escape the tunnel of darkness, the tunnel of ideas.
The boundless is the vast.
The no-mind is the universe mind.

INTERPRETATION

"If there is someone who hears of the principle of *The Diamond Sutra* and its merits and experiences neither astonishment, nor fear, nor intimidation, then this will be a truly special person, and such a person will practice the notionless charity of which the Tathāgata speaks.

"Subhuti! By 'pāramitā of forbearance,' the Tathāgata is referring to having let go of even the slightest trace of having suppressed desire [the culmination of forbearance practice]. For Subhuti! When I long ago experienced the pain of having my limbs hacked away by the King of Kalinga, I remained in that realm truly devoid of the four misleading concepts. Had I had even the slightest trace of those notions while my body was being cut to pieces, profound anger would have arisen within me.

"Subhuti! I was also devoid of the four misleading concepts when I cultivated the Way over five hundred lifetimes as a hermit practitioner of asceticism.

"The bodhisattva must engage in practice toward leaving behind all names and signs and achieving the great Way that is free of notions. Practitioners must therefore not fixate with their minds on any sensory conditions. They should practice charitable acts without clinging to any ideas or notions within their mind."

True Charity Is Given Unconditionally

Among the Mahāyāna dharma instructions of the Buddha, there is one called the "Six Pāramitās." This instruction is one that many Buddhists have adopted as a standard for living and endeavored to put into practice. The Six Pāramitās, or perfections, are charitable giving, right conduct, forbearance, absorption, diligence, and wisdom. We are exhorted to cross over to the ideal world of the buddha kingdom through devoted practice of these six perfections. The Buddha focuses on two representative virtues: charitable giving and forbearance.

First, there is the pāramitā of charitable giving. This means giving benefits to others in spiritual, physical, and material terms without conditions. When we happen to find ourselves helping others, we ordinary humans and sentient beings always have the expectation that others should help us as much as we have helped them. This is a kind of conditional charity. This charity with notions attached is ultimately the seed of torment.

We are pursued by a myriad of discriminating minds because of shadows in the mind. We ask, "Why are you not helping me as I helped you?" We calculate relative amounts and conclude that we received less than we offered, and we think of ourselves as special for having given our aid.

The charity of which the Buddha speaks is pure charity without expectations. It is true love, and an expression of the mind of mercy.

Only through this kind of charity, he says, can we enter the buddha world. Only this kind of charity is charity based on not leaving the self-nature, and the mercy of the buddha who acts without false notions.

Forbearance Without the Idea of Forbearance

Next, there is the pāramitā of forbearance. The true buddha pāramitā of forbearance means forbearing with no mind, with no trace of the notion that we are forbearing now. Generally, forbearance takes one of two forms. The first is forbearance with some purpose. In such cases, we actually experience difficulties stemming from our forbearance later on after we have achieved our desired result. The second is forbearance without notions. We must understand that true forbearance consists of forbearing without the notion of forbearance, with an acceptance that things are as they should be.

Jesus Christ traveled around delivering many teachings to deliver the Jewish people. Yet certain Jews gave false testimony against him and sought his death on the cross. The governor at the time wished to spare him, and put the question to the public. Still, these Jewish people are said to have conspired together and ordered his death by crucifixion. How must Jesus have felt at this moment? As the nails were hammered into his hands, he prayed, "My God, why hast

Thou forsaken me?"

"All things are possible for Thee," he said. "Take this cup away from me. Yet not what I will, but what Thou wilt."

How could he have delivered such a prayer if he did not have a mind without notions?

When Śākyamuni was a hermit practitioner of asceticism, he endured the dismemberment of his body at the hands of the King of Kalinga without false notions.

In his dharma instruction, Master Taesan asked what the King of Kalinga represented to sentient beings. The answer, he said, was sensory conditions. When our mind is stolen from us by good music, nice clothes, and things of that sort, this is none other than the King of Kalinga. Even at this moment, sensory conditions are stealing and scattering our true mind. We must therefore understand that sensory conditions are the King of Kalinga and withstand them appropriately so that we may preserve our true mind.

You may have, among your affinities, one or more that are a source of constant torment to your mind. You must engage in practice toward seeing them not as the King of Kalinga but as buddhas to whom you should make buddha offerings, and you should also engage in the practice of forbearance.

Every person, when engaged in some affair, will often encounter an opposing faction. Even when we wish to do good works, there is certain to be someone who gets in our way. In the past, such cases were dealt with by suppression. The past was an age of suppressing the minions of Māra. Today, in contrast, we must think of a way to quietly appease the demons without suppressing them, and thereby to overcome them wisely. For today is an era of "resolving Māra."

Conversely, I hope that you will consider your understanding of the King of Kalinga. I hope that you will ask yourself, "Who is suffering on account of me? Who is troubled by me?" I hope that you will at least become someone who, as a person cultivating the Way, considers whether you should be anyone's King of Kalinga. You should avoid causing trouble to others by engaging in sincere forbearance practice.

The forbearance that contains the idea of our forbearing,

It is forbearance practice

where we enter the pit of fire carrying gunpowder.

The forbearance without need for forbearance,

the forbearance where forbearance is sweet,

The black cloud and cushion of thorns

become a bellows furnace for forging the buddha.

"Subhuti! The bodhisattva must perform acts of generosity so that all sentient beings benefit in this way. Thus, none of the names and concepts of which the Tathāgata spoke are constant and eternal notions, nor do all sentient beings remain as sentient beings forever."

Do Not Abide Even in the Buddha's Doctrine

Because the Buddha is so tremendously thoughtful, he repeatedly emphasizes that we must wash away our preconceptions and our lingering notions about what we have done, and help others with a clean mind-ground. The Buddha's words have been organized into doctrine and systematized as the Six Pāramitās, the Four Noble Truths, the Eightfold Path, and the Threefold Study of precepts, absorption, and wisdom. But we must not allow ourselves to be caught and obstructed by the Buddha's doctrine—that is, by the dharma notion.

When we begin our practice, we hew strictly to the dharma line based on the doctrine of the Buddha. At the next stage, however, we must gain freedom even from that dharma line. The sequence is similar to the way in which an airplane must first race along the runway before soaring into the unobstructed ether.

This is the case for a sentient being suffering from the five desires and defilements, for he has not practiced the buddhadharma. He must understand that when he enters the path of practice and exerts himself intently, yesterday's sentient being becomes tomorrow's buddha, and he must thereby escape from the framework of fixed ideas.

In this world, there is nothing that does not change. The only thing that does not change is the truth of change—all is a state of change. Your mind right now is changing. My mind is changing. The heavens and earth are changing, and the relationship between you and me is changing. When we realize for certain this fact of change, fixed notions of "You are this sort of person" disappear, as does our mind of expectation from others. If we are fated to change, we should change toward becoming buddhas, taking as our model the Buddha's doctrine. Just as we treat the people we encounter with care as buddhas, eliminating fixed notions and preconceptions of "gentle" and "hateful," so we must improve the relationship between those persons and ourselves into one of buddhas, of mutual aid and assistance.

"Subhuti! The Tathāgata speaks the truth, speaks with sincerity, speaks consistently, and is not one to speak empty or mysterious words."

The Buddha's Pride and the Ordinary Human's Pride

Some may read about the Buddha saying, "I am one who speaks only the truth," and think to themselves, "So the Buddha, too, is boastful," or "The Buddha, too, has notions." But the Buddha's words here were not uttered out of boastfulness or notions.

When we boast, we are filled with notions and are unable to suppress the mind to boast. The Buddha, however, spoke with a mind free of notions in order to instill sure faith in sentient beings and to educate them. It may therefore be difficult on the surface to distinguish the buddha from the ordinary human and sentient being.

Because both the buddha and the ordinary human or sentient being boast, it is impossible to know the difference before looking within, and it is difficult to tell the false enlightened master from the true one. Many ordinary humans lie because of their circumstances, and engage in habitual exaggeration. They inflate their characteristics to promote themselves to others. Few people speak the unvarnished truth. We practitioners must speak without falsehood and with a basis in fact at all times, and we must refrain in particular from saying things that are damaging to others' mind of faith or that alienate others. Our words must necessarily be things that improve ourselves and others, and that transmit the buddhadharma.

Speech is inevitably an expression of the mind and a measure of character. We should examine our own words carefully so that we speak according to the facts from a mind free of notions.

INTERPRETATION

"Subhuti! The dharma practiced by the Tathāgata is an abstruse realm that has no real image and is not empty, one that truly cannot be understood through language and thought.

"Subhuti! When the bodhisattva performs acts of generosity while fixing the mind on a certain dharma, he is similar to a person who has entered the darkness and cannot see. And when he acts without fixating on any mind, it is as though his eye can distinguish all the different colors reflected in the bright rays of the sun."

The Truth Without Real or False Images

What did the Buddha realize when he experienced right enlightenment under the bodhi tree? It was the mind that is neither substantial nor empty. This is also the Way and principle that governs the universe. This Way and principle of the universe, our original mind, is tranquil and empty of even the smallest speck, so that it cannot be described in words. It admits not even a trace of nonbeing and is free from all values of "good" or "bad," a realm that is not and yet, because it is not, is not not.

For this reason, it was called the "insubstantial" realm, but it is a realm that is marvelously bright, brighter than the sun, warm and merciful, higher than the warm grace of parents, a realm "without emptiness" that is utterly filled with the ultimate grace and creative transformations.

Having experienced right enlightenment to the truth and practiced with the truth that is neither insubstantial nor empty as his standard for living, the Buddha attained freedom from all sensory conditions and the wisdom to know the best way of living for the universe and human life, as well as the great mercy and great dharma power to console and share with sentient beings. This is referred to as "Anuttara-Samyak-Sambodhi."

Ultimately, Anuttara-Samyak-Sambodhi could be described as the culmination of the Buddha, and it lies entirely in awakening to the truth that is neither insubstantial nor empty.

Fixation Leads to Darkening

I will use an example for the instruction that states, "When the mind is fixated, it is darkened, and when it is free of dwelling, this is right vision." There is a railroad that passes through the Dongsan neighborhood in Iksan. One day, a straw hat flew onto the tracks while a train was passing by. An old man who appeared to be the owner saw only the hat and raced onto the tracks. He was unable to get out of the way of the train, and he ended up being struck by it. The man had fixated on the straw hat and failed to see a train. Now, you may read this and think, "I would never do such a thing." But while the forms may differ, human lives are riddled with mistakes owing to fixation.

You may have fixated on an affinity and experienced the failure to see anything else. And when you think well of an affinity, you may fail to see its negative aspects. This is not right vision. I recall one person who saw the nature and said, "Now I understand that there is a garden at our home." In other words, prior to this realization the person did not see the garden as a garden, and now the garden appeared as a garden. The Founding Master, too, is said to have realized his beard and fingernails were too long and trimmed them only after experiencing great enlightenment. Things become clear once we have the mind that is free of dwelling.

I will mention one other story. It happened when I was living in the Wonnam neighborhood of Seoul. It was a rainy day, and I was traveling along a side street when I saw a woman standing in front of a wall. She was striking the wall and crying, "This is my house!" I thought I had seen a ghost. When I looked closer, I saw that she was a person, but one wearing ragged clothes who was apparently out of her mind. Later, I inquired about the reason for this and learned that she had previously been the owner of the house. Her husband had lost it through gambling. I was told that she had worked very hard and struggled to buy that house. How great her attachment to that house must have been!

After that, I was told, she had gone mad. Ever since then, she traveled to the lost house whenever the weather was poor and pounded on the wall, crying, "Give me back my house." Unaware of the circumstances, the new owner chased her away. Consider for a moment how the woman arrived at this state. This is how fearsome a thing fixation is. Where would this woman's soul go if she were to die in this state? It would hover around the home in an effort to reclaim it.

We, too, are like this, albeit to varying degrees. We are darkened by fixation. Consider whether you are truly living well right now. In order to avoid living a darkened life from too much fixation and succumbing to an unwholesome destiny, we need to awaken to the realm without fixations and act without fixations. We can only proceed on the right path when we have right vision.

"If there exists a virtuous man or woman in the coming world who studies and practices *The Diamond Sutra*, the Tathāgata will see and know all through his wisdom, offering protection and encouragement so that he or she realizes the limitless merits of the buddha."

The Buddha Who Sees and Knows Our Mind

After many, many years of mind-practice, we gain a clear understanding of principle. We realize that the principle by which the seasons cycle and the principle by which a person experiences eternal life through the process of birth, aging, sickness, and death are one and the same, and we gain an understanding of the sequence of change in all things and their constituent elements. There is nothing in this world that escapes the embrace of this principle. Once we awaken to it, we can apply it in observing the world and discerning its process of rising and falling, prosperity and decline. We can also determine immediately whether our own household is in a process of decay or flourishing.

If we continue practicing with the desires, defilements, and idle thoughts within our mind, we become bodies of numinous nature like spotless crystal. Once restored, this spiritual nature is somewhat like a clear mirror, showing the full aspect of objects when we reflect them in it. A kind of radiant spiritual sense emerges. When our understanding of principle combines with this spiritual sense, this is ordinarily described as a penetration of the numinous spirit, the culmination of the great wisdom called "complete and utter mastery." We must believe and understand that the buddhas of the past, present, and future experienced this culmination of great wisdom, possessing the mercy to clearly read the minds of their followers, offer the right prescription for them, and guide them on the path toward becoming buddhas.

There is one thing that we must be wary of, however. The person who spends a long time engaged only in practice toward Cultivating the Spirit or practice with serenity and the elimination of idle thoughts may gain temporary knowledge of the minds of others through the emergence of superpowers. He may temporarily understand changes in the weather or the political situation in the world, and he may gain partial knowledge of others' destinies. But such cases are called false spiritual openings. In the orthodox order of the Way, this is called a wicked path, a mistaken road. For the kind of superpowers that are opened up simply because the spirit has become clear are temporary and partial, and such a person cannot teach about principles because he does not understand them.

These superpowers will grow gradually darker through continued use. Furthermore, desires emerge and the gateway of superpowers closes as we receive compensation and respect from others. As time passes, we come to speak falsehoods and to deceive, leading to wickedness that causes great harm to ourselves and others. We must distinguish properly between superpowers and the previously explained numinous spirit of the buddha.

CHAPTER XV

THE TATHĀGATA SEES AND KNOWS ALL

The Merits of Upholding the Sutra

So it is, people eat rice to live.

What does the roc take as its food?

Zhaozhou's "nought" or Yunmen's pancake?

Oh, wings of the great phoenix beating atop Mt. Sumeru.

"Subhuti! Even when the virtuous man or woman gives any many bodies as there are grains of sand in the Ganges in the morning, gives any many bodies as there are grains of sand in the Ganges in the afternoon, and gives as many bodies as there are grains of sand in the Ganges again in the evening, performing charitable service for hundreds of thousands of tens thousands of ten millions of kalpas in this way, the blessings of another person who hears this scripture and does not defy the mind of faith will exceed even those. How much greater for him who writes by brush, accepts and upholds, reads and recites it and speaks it to others.

Subhuti! In summary, the merits of this sutra are unimaginable, immeasurable, and boundless. The Tathāgata therefore teaches it to those who have set the aspiration of the Mahāyāna, to those who have set the aspiration of the Supreme Vehicle.

If someone accepts and upholds it, reads and recites it, and teaches it to others, the Tathāgata will know all and see all, and that person will achieve attainment of merits that are entirely unfathomable, indescribable, boundless, and unimaginable.

Such people are said to be carrying the Anuttara-Samyak-

Sambodhi of the Tathāgata. For Subhuti! He who delights in the small dharma will fixate on views of the self, the person, the sentient being, and long life, and he will be unable to hear, read, and recite this sutra and explain it to others.

Subhuti! In every place where this sutra is present, all the heavenly beings and asuras of all the worlds will give offerings.

You should understand this. This place will become a stupa and shrine. All will venerate it, perform worship, and surround it, adorning it with flowers and incense."

Focus on

In this section, the Buddha explains that when we read, write, and practice *The Diamond Sutra* with utmost sincerity and communicate it to others, the merits are far higher and greater than even those of dedicating countless lifetimes to charitable service. The Tathāgata says here that he sees and knows all about the accumulation of merits by his students. We will learn how this is possible, and we will also study why the practitioner engaged in Theravāda practice cannot understand the Way and principle of *The Diamond Sutra*. In addition, we will examine the difference between the Mahāyāna and Theravāda.

"Subhuti! Even when the person who has produced the kindest of minds gives as many bodies as there are grains of sand in the Ganges in the morning, gives as many bodies as there are grains of sand in the Ganges in the afternoon, and gives as many bodies as there are grains of sand in the Ganges again in the evening, performing charitable service for ten million kalpas in this way, another person who hears this *Diamond Sutra* and produces a mind of faith without denying it will enjoy greater merits than he. And indescribably boundless will be the merits coming to him who writes, recites, and practices *The Diamond Sutra* and interprets it for others."

Where Do Thoughts Come From?

There was a Zen master named Jiexian who devoted much study to the sutras. He had a student under him by the name of Xinchan. Xinchan observed his teacher and came to the conclusion that he only read the sutras, without doing any training of the mind. "I'll never see the nature and attain buddhahood under this teacher," he said, and went off to awaken to the Way under Baizhang. Later on, he recalled Jiexian, the teacher who had prized him, and he returned to the temple. He decided to become a student again as in the old days. One day, he was bathing the older monk. As he washed Jiexian's back, Xinchang muttered, "The dharma hall is wonderful, but the Buddha has no numinous efficacy!"

"What did you say?" asked Jiexian.

"The Buddha has no numinous efficacy, but he radiates the light!" replied Xinchan.

The mind is something inexhaustibly replete, yet we do not understand this aspect of our mind. So as Xinchan bathed the old monk, he said, "The body is fine and healthy, yet he does not understand his own mind."

There was also a man long ago named Layman Pang. He was a married man, with a child and a large fortune. After hearing the buddhadharma, he became concerned. "When am I ever to attain Buddhahood if I spend my life counting money?" he said. He made up his mind to divide up his assets, and all of his relatives came running. Things grew very complicated. Finally, Layman Pang loaded all of his fortune onto a boat and sent it floating off onto Dongting Lake. After that, it is said, he committed himself to mind-practice.

One day, he emerged from seated meditation singing a song with the words, "The hundred blades of grass are the same as the bright shining meaning of the enlightened master." He was enjoying himself when his daughter (who had also studied a great deal) heard him and said, "This yellow-toothed fellow says all kinds of crazy things!"

Hearing this, Layman Pang asked, "So how would you say it?" He was asking how she would describe that realm.

She, too, said, "The hundred blades of grass are the same as the bright shining meaning of the enlightened master."

The theme of this story is how the hundred blades of grass and the mind of the enlightened master are alike. Are they? Are they different?

Blessings, wisdom, and mercy arise as a result of the functioning of the mind. The mind that creates blessings is a kind and generous mind, the seed of virtue and the seed of blessings. Where do their roots extend? Conversely, when a mind commits wicked deeds, its roots lie in greed, anger, and delusion, do they not? Those three poisons are indeed the root of wickedness. Yet there is a place where both the roots of good and the roots of evil are embedded. Once we understand the mind-field where goodness has its roots, we have discovered the source of all sources of blessings and merits. The merit of teaching this is the greatest of merits.

When Merits Actually Bring Harm

We enjoy the blessings that come after we have worked to create merits. But when we have accumulated merits that are not recognized, we become angry. And when we create merits without understanding of the truth, we may grow lazy or arrogant due to the blessings that come our way, or we may grow angry and suffer the torments of hell because we are not recognized.

We may become greedy, unable to content ourselves with our material abundance and an abundance of blessings in our affinities, and we may rise to anger when things do not proceed as we hope. We may also suffer when others do not recognize our material wealth. Even when we enjoy the blessings that come from accumulating merits with material things, we are prone to actually becoming slaves of material things, trapped by ideas and living in a sea of suffering. How could this possibly be the best way for a human to live his life?

When we study the truth, the Dharmakāya, and *The Diamond Sutra*, we become someone who can use his mind as he wishes and, at the ultimate stage, someone who creates and commands many merits. We ride about on merits as though riding a bicycle.

Long ago, there was a famous poet named Bai Letian. One day, he traveled to a temple with an attendant. He met a Zen monk there by the name of Daolin. Daolin, a somewhat fastidious sort, had made a place for himself at the top of a tree, where he practiced seated meditation. This is how he came to be known as "Daolin" ("way forest"), or "Niaolin" ("bird forest").

As he looked up, Bai saw the monk in a precarious position at the top of his tree. "Venerable One, that's dangerous!" he cried.

From his perch atop the tree, Daolin looked at Bai and told the man on the ground, "Now, that's dangerous. Watch out!"

"I have the heavens over my head and the ground beneath my feet," said Bai. "What's dangerous about that?"

In response, Daolin called down, "The anger has not entirely cooled in your head. Your mind is constantly floating and agitated. You may encounter some misfortune. That's why you're in danger. I am always in the ultimate bliss of absorption, and remain in ultimate bliss no matter who comes to talk to me. You are one who will rise to anger if someone fails to acknowledge your words, and you are in danger because the knowledge and emotions in your head do not cool."

At that moment, it is said, Bai Letian took refuge with the monk.

Consider what this story is saying. We may experience some small happiness, yet someone can come along and upset us by defying our will, leading us to explode in anger. How can this be called living well?

I knew of someone who hired a caretaker to guard his summer home. But the caretaker did not do the cleaning that the owner desired. Furious, the owner reprimanded the caretaker for his mistake and called him up periodically to check. As I considered this person, it seemed to me as though the villa had consumed his mind. His mind was experiencing great torment because of it.

When we fail to obtain the Way and principle of *The Diamond Sutra*, we become slaves to material things, slaves to honors, bound to praise for our beauty, or our concept of ourselves as thinkers. We should therefore appreciate the meaning of this chapter all the more and give it deep consideration.

> The mind of "pride" is the seed
> of ten million transgressions and torments.
> The mind of repentance after misdeeds
> is the seed of the good mind.
> If we cannot clip the tail of ideas
> even after our efforts toward success,
> The buddha life of no mind and great peace is unimaginable.

INTERPRETATION

"Subhuti! In short, the merits of this *Diamond Sutra* are without limit, cannot be measured in any way, and cannot be discussed through ideas. The Tathāgata therefore teaches it to Buddhist disciples who seek to practice the will of the Mahāyāna, to the disciples who seek to practice the supreme will of the Mahāyāna."

A Word to the Bodhisattva of the Highest State

The truth of *The Diamond Sutra* was delivered for the highest of spiritual capacities. It is said that when they awaken to this truth, ordinary humans and beings make an instantaneous leap to become tathāgatas. We can understand this to mean that it was a scripture for teaching the highest level of student because its merits were that great.

Someone once gave me a big wooden bowl. With such bowls, a smaller bowl goes inside of a larger one. Strangely, the dish that I received had a larger bowl that went into a smaller one. Have you seen it? I see it every morning. Every time, the smaller one goes into the larger one, with room left to spare. Have you not seen it? All of you possess it. This is what *The Diamond Sutra* teaches. No matter how much you use it, it keeps coming with room to spare. It truly is an amazing thing.

I have a son. I raised him well, and he commands a vast array of talents. You can use this for a lifetime and still it remains. You can use it for an eternity of lifetimes, and still it remains. You can become buddha, and still it remains. Do you have that sort of son? If you train yourself well, this is something extraordinary. All of you have a son who can be your son, your grandfather, or your mother or daughter at times. All of you have that wooden bowl.

We need to awaken to this realm, adopt it as our own, and dwell with it at all times. Only that way can we truly achieve serenity in all things, experiencing comfort in our mind as we conduct affairs externally, and becoming someone who needs no help, someone who commands the world.

INTERPRETATION

"If a student of Buddhism reads and recites this scripture, and if he truly puts it into practice and teaches it to others, he will know all and see all with the wisdom eye of the Tathāgata. The merits to be gained are infinite, immeasurable, and without boundary, and he will come to achieve inestimable character and blessings. For this buddhist disciple will be entrusted with the mission of communicating the unsurpassed great Way of the Tathāgata. For the person who practices the dharma with form and discovers pleasure within that framework is bound in his life by views of 'myself,' and views of 'you,' views of 'sentient beings' and 'long life.' He cannot receive, carry, read, and recite

The Diamond Sutra; still less can he put it into practice."

The Mind That Is Not Sacred

One word from a president has great significance in deciding the affairs of a country, but the responsibility of teaching all living creatures and imparting the morality for delivering them is of far greater significance. For this reason, the Buddha is called the great enlightened teacher of the three worlds. He bears responsibility for delivering all sentient beings of the world of desire, the world of form, and the formless world. The person who understands the Way and principle of *The Diamond Sutra* assumes this responsibility. When a person is unaware of the Way and principle of *The Diamond Sutra* and practices with a fixation on a kind of dharma of action, believing his own religion to be superior, he will hear the Way and principle and actually deny them, saying that they cannot be true.

Long ago, Bodhidharma preached of "only that mind realm that cannot be understood." He explained that it was a realm that had shed even sacredness. A monk who had devoted himself solely to intently studying the precepts said, "The Buddha is sacred, and the realm of nature is sacred, and by saying they are not, Bodhidharma has committed a grave violation of the precepts." He ordered Bodhidharma to take poison. In the process of focusing on practice with a kind of notion in the mind, he failed to recognize a great monk and committed the transgression of poisoning him.

Ordinary humans and sentient beings produce minds of good and bad according to their desires. The person who has cultivated seeds of good through cultivation of the Way comes to fixate on that good and produce minds of good and bad accordingly. Someone who has cultivated the spirit of benefiting others as a seed of good will see the selfish person and experience chaos and loathing in his mind. Someone who has cultivated the mind of kindness as a seed of good will argue that the mind of good is supreme and adopt himself as a benchmark, looking down on other people who do not possess good minds. And when a bad mind emerges from within himself, he torments himself for going against the seed of good. The Way and principle of *The Diamond Sutra* teaches that we must regard even these good minds as thieves and strive to reach the no-mind state where even they are absent.

Previously, I discussed cultivating the splendor of the buddha land. We cultivate it with the no-mind, adorning it with the true mind of faith, the kind mind, and the mind of grace. But when we cultivate it with the mind of charitable donation and the mind of faith without knowing how to achieve no-mind, we become stubborn and freedom eludes us.

In Chinese philosophy, Buddhism is criticized as a religion that corrupts morality. The argument is that it is a religion without a father or a king. This slander comes from an ignorance of the deep and high realm of the buddha mind. They cast aspersions on Buddhism because of their unawareness of the high state of discriminations based in the dharma of no-action, in which we use all things properly from a transcendent mind beyond even awakening and practice.

If you push on and on through the reed forest,
You meet a beautiful vast blue sea.
That wide open void beyond the sea's edge,
Register the address of that void in your mind.
The landscape, the plants, the defilements
will become crystal beads.

INTERPRETATION

"Subhuti! When this *Diamond Sutra* is present somewhere, the heavenly beings and asuras will know all about it and perform offerings.

It will be a buddha place where they hover about as though laying offerings at a stupa of the Buddha, performing respectful courtesies, adorning it with flowers, and burning incense."

The Religious Foundation of Our Cultural Heritage

Back when the Buddha was alive, there was no paper, and so people would cleave sections of bamboo for their records, or treat broad leaves and write upon them. One would have had to have a lot of money to be able to write on bamboo or treated leaves, and it would have been a very rare and valuable endeavor. For this reason, the place where the vast text of something like *The Diamond Sutra* was written and recited, and where its contents were understood, practiced, and taught to others, would have to have been either a temple or a place where eminent and virtuous monks lived. The place where *The Diamond Sutra* was present would therefore have circulating in it a clear, radiant, and warm energy, an energy that would have immediately become a refuge for people.

It is not only a dwelling place for the visible living creatures in this universe. There are also the worlds of unseen heavenly spirits, and innumerable asuras roaming about as mere souls without bodies. Such spirits and ghosts possess very keen senses, and since they, too, hope to progress and hear the supreme dharma instructions of the Buddha, they travel to the place where *The Diamond Sutra* exists and leave offerings.

The place of the Buddha and his high students was consecrated as sacred ground, a place of worship and offerings. Because of this truth, all of the cultural heritage in human history originated and developed in religion. As we all know, music developed from praise for the Buddha and adoration of his thoughts and life, as did murals and painting, while architecture was a benediction to praise this spirit of the Buddha.

> Many people prize and adore their cultural heritage
> But do not know to find the sacred meaning that imbues the ruins.
> Sentient beings express gratitude for the rising sun and
> praise the beauty of the rising moon,
> But do not know to find the face
> that makes the sun rise and the moon set.

CHAPTER XVI

REDUCING KARMA FROM PREVIOUS LIVES

Capably Cleansing Karmic Obstructions

The traveler who roams countless worlds far from home,
Tracks of tears, stains of blood with every fold in his clothes.
Send them floating away in the flowing waters of the dragon's pond.
May you now dance naked with the dragon and phoenix.

"Subhuti! Even as the virtuous man and woman accept and uphold, read and recite this sutra,

those who are despised by others will fall on the evil path because of transgressive karma from past lives. But by accepting poor treatment in this world, their transgressive karma from past lives is extinguished, and they will attain Anuttara-Samyak-Sambodhi.

Subhuti! I recall from infinite asamkhyeya kalpas of past lives that I met, honored, revered, and served 84 million myriads of nayutas of buddhas before Dīpaṃkara Buddha without omitting a single one.

If someone is able to accept and uphold, read and recite this sutra in the later end times, the merits obtained will be such that the merits of my offerings to all buddhas will not amount to one-hundredth of it, nor could they be likened to even one-thousandth of a ten-thousandth of a hundred-millionth, or any number.

Subhuti! Were I to speak of all the merits to be gained when the virtuous man and woman in the later end times is capable of reading and reciting this sutra, receiving and upholding it, a tumult would arise in the mind of the listener, doubt would arise like a fox, and he would not believe.

Subhuti! You should understand this. The meaning of this sutra cannot be imagined, nor can the karmic rewards to be gained."

Focus on

This section teaches us that when we believe in and practice the content of this scripture, the resulting merits can reduce even the heavy karmic power that comes from our deeds in past lives (through our acceptance of others' contempt in this life). In this chapter, we will learn about bad karma and examine how we can reduce transgressive karma from previous lives by practicing *The Diamond Sutra*. We will also examine the difference in merits between practice with and without knowledge of the Way and principle of *The Diamond Sutra*.

"Subhuti! Even as the virtuous man and woman read and recite *The Diamond Sutra* and put it into practice, those who are shunned by others are destined to fall on the evil path because of transgressive karma from past lives. But by accepting poor treatment today, they come to realize the unsurpassed great Way while being subjected to fewer karmic obstacles from past lives."

Reducing Karma by Studying *The Diamond Sutra*

When a person acts through the functioning of his mind, body, and mouth, the results do not manifest themselves straight away, but are stored for a certain period of time. When the content stored away is good, it is called "good karma," and when bad content is stored it is called "bad karma." Just as the food that we eat is digested and stored away in the liver, secreted to the different organs to provide energy as needed, so all of human behavior is stored away in the mind. This is called karma.

Because this karma has the power to act, we use the term "karmic power." This power is concealed within all people. In previous lives, we may have had a relationship of fondness with someone, or one of loathing. As a result of this functioning, we meet that person again through the karmic power of love or resentment. The karma of mistreatment described in *The Diamond Sutra* results from our committing bad deeds against others out of ignorance of the truth, or from the karmic power of bad habits lingering in our mind because of bad deeds that we have committed.

Even with this karmic power of mistreatment, there exists a principle whereby we can minimize its weight through *The Diamond Sutra* by aspiring to the sutra, which may be called the supreme essence of the buddhadharma—to receive, uphold, read, and serve it with utmost sincerity, and adopt it as our standard in building dharma power. We can do so even when we have committed transgressions out of ignorance in a past life, when desire has led us to knowingly create the kind of bad karma that leads to death at another's hands, or when we have generated the karma that results in a body that is not whole.

To elaborate on my previous explanation, karma is divided into two types, depending on where it is stored. One could be called "self-karma," referring to the storage of habits and talents in our mind, while the other could be called "other-directed karma," referring to what is planted in others' minds as we affect them with our actions.

The fog of self-karma can be extinguished when we dedicatedly practice the Way and principle of the Buddha's *Diamond Sutra*. But the other karma buried in other people cannot be extinguished, for the right to take retaliation lies with those people. Even in this case, however, the party subject to retribution can reduce his misfortune to about 50 to 60 percent by influencing the other's vicious mind of retaliation through *Diamond Sutra* practice with the utmost sincerity. We can also receive far less when we bear the retaliation with a placid mind, knowing that it is the result of what we created in previous lives.

By aspiring to *The Diamond Sutra* and practicing with utmost sincerity after adopting it as a standard, we can dissolve the karma that comes from previous lives. By understanding the principle, we can minimize to the level of mere mistreatment even the great transgressive karma that would result in death at another's hands, or a body that is not whole.

Lately, people live with backpacks on their backs,
Carrying them around wherever they go, even when they sleep.
The newly born and the aged alike carry bundles of karma.
What is concealed in that karma pocket
that has built up over the ages?
Unsavory skills, great talents, nasty natures, good natures,
All manner of junk, and the *mani* pearl as well.
You ascending the mountain, you journeying through eternal life,
Put down your karma-pocket backpack and rest a while.

"Subhuti! I recall from my infinite past lives that I revered and served the buddhadharma in the orders of 84 million myriads of nayutas of buddhas before Dīpaṃkara Buddha, and never once was this effort in vain. If others receive, carry, read, and recite this scripture in the coming end times, the merits will be incomparably greater than those of my offering to all the buddhas in previous lives without knowledge of the sutra's principle."

The Soul Is Eternal, Neither Arising Nor Ceasing

It is impossible not to marvel at the fact that the Buddha knew all about things from his past lives, tens of thousands of years before. We ordinary humans and sentient beings lived through past lives, but we are unaware of it. Foolishly, we deny and ignore our past lifetimes, and we are naturally unaware of the existence of a next life. This is true foolishness.

We living creatures possess a soul that lives through changing bodies over an infinite expanse of time. Our soul is not something that was born somewhere, nor does it ever go away. We believe it to have a beginning and an end. This is a mistake. There is only an endless cycle without beginning or end, every finish connecting with a new start, eternally existing. We may be a Jang in this life because we encountered a father in Mr. Jang, but our father may have been Mr. Kim in a previous life, and we may be a Lee in the next, if we encounter a father in Mr. Lee.

With his numinous eye of wisdom, the Buddha tells us of previous lives from millions of years before. The person who lacks awareness will regard this as legend and refuse to believe it.

It is not only Śākyamuni Buddha who lived for millions of years. All of you reading this also lived for untold millions of years. You are simply unaware of it because your numinous eye is not open. We need to work diligently to instill in ourselves the ability to clarify our numinous nature and know the past, present, and future.

It appears that the Buddha himself studied merely with the mind of faith before encountering Dīpaṃkara Buddha. Because Dīpaṃkara Buddha taught him the principle of the self-nature that is the unsurpassed great path, he finally became a presiding sage through practice with the self-nature realm as his standard.

The difference in merits between cultivation with and without awareness of the right path of practice is the difference between heaven and earth. Imagine what a difference there is in solving a math problem with and without knowledge of the rules of multiplication. How can one ever attain buddhahood if he thinks that all there is to practice is reading the sutras, performing charitable service, and upholding the precepts?

Only by discovering and training the three jewels of the self-nature that exist in our mind—the pure Dharmakāya Buddha, the perfectly wise Sambhogakāya Buddha, and the Nirmaṇakāya Buddha that grants charity through ten billion incarnations—do we attain buddhahood and gain the unlimited capability to deliver sentient beings. In the end, we must believe that there exists within us a true teacher capable of teaching what a teacher of phenomena (or character) cannot. We must find it and train it if we are to become a great individual of extraordinary capabilities, a teacher of humans and heavenly beings, and a great enlightened teacher of the three worlds.

INTERPRETATION

"Subhuti! Were I to speak of all the merits to be gained when the virtuous man and woman of the returning end times read and recite this sutra, receive and carry it, a tumult would arise in the mind of the listener, doubt would arise like a fox, and he would not believe.

"Subhuti! The profound meaning of this sutra is beyond comprehension, and the rewards to be gained are unimaginably great, high, and eternal.

You must believe and awaken to this."

Becoming a Figure for the Global Village Age

We know nothing of what is to come even a few days from now, yet the Buddha, back in the right dharma period, prophesied a declining dharma age that was at least several thousand years away. While the people born in this age may not be aware of this, someone born fifty years ago will have an acute sense of how the world today has changed completely. How much more impossible it would be for the ordinary person, back in the time the Buddha was active many thousands of years ago, to imagine how much things would change between then and now. Even if he had predicted and explained all about the current times to his students, few would have believed him.

From reading *The Diamond Sutra*, one can sense that the Buddha was already predicting the events of the degenerate age, preparing for them, and experiencing concern for them.

The past was characterized by local cultures in the broad sense. Little interchange took place among the Christian, Islamic, and Buddhist cultural spheres. It was therefore possible to speak of this time as the age of local culture, or of local cultural spheres. But the future culture that is to unfold in the days ahead is to be a "global village" culture where the whole world becomes one—the age of an all-encompassing cultural sphere, the cultural sphere of the circle. The past age of local cultural spheres is receding, and the age of a vast global village cultural sphere uniting the entire world is at hand. And as time passes, I believe there will be an age of a universal cultural sphere.

Religious pronouncements were also local in the past. In the future, however, religious doctrine will have to possess an unprecedented, vast framework that is global, equal, and interwoven. This will be the age of sages, of buddhas who view the entire world as their home and all humankind as their family members. This, I believe, is what the Buddha predicted. He foresaw that boundless blessings would come to one who understood the principle of the diamond self-nature and trained his mind nature in it. Readers, let us vigorously train our diamond self-nature to become the one whom the Buddha predicted.

The sentient being wanders, having lost its buddha.
The buddha finds and uses his buddha.
The Diamond Sutra gestures toward our self-buddha.
Do you see your buddha now? Do you understand now?
Ha ha, hm hm.

CHAPTER XVII

I WITHOUT I
No Self in the Ultimate Realm

At the edge of the void, there is nowhere to stick a gimlet,

Nor is there a gimlet that can be stuck in the place absent even of the void.

How peculiar it is.

Why are there clouds and rain, frost and snow in an empty sky?

In the end, it is always Buddha—the long-lived Sun Face Buddha,

or the short-lived Moon Face Buddha.

At this time, Subhuti said to the Buddha, "World Honored One! If the virtuous man and virtuous woman set the aspiration of achieving Anuttara-Samyak-Sambodhi, where are their minds to abide, and how are they to subdue wicked minds?"

Said the Buddha to Subhuti, "The virtuous man or woman who has set the aspiration of achieving Anuttara-Samyak-Sambodhi must produce the following mind:

'I will necessarily deliver all sentient beings,' he will say. 'And after I have finished delivering all sentient beings, there will in reality be no actual deliverance of even one sentient being.'

For if a bodhisattva possesses conceptions of the self, the person, the sentient being, and long life, he is not a bodhisattva.

For Subhuti! It is not because there is any dharma in reality that one produces the aspiration of achieving Anuttara-Samyak-Sambodhi.

Subhuti! What do you think? Did the Tathāgata obtain Anuttara-Samyak-Sambodhi because there was a dharma in the presence of Dīpaṃkara Buddha?"

"No, World Honored One! From what I have understood of the Buddha's teaching, the Buddha did not obtain Anuttara-Samyak-Sambodhi because there was a dharma in the presence of Dīpaṃkara Buddha.

Said the Buddha, "Yes, it is just so. Subhuti! In truth, there is no dharma such that the Tathāgata obtained Anuttara-Samyak-Sambodhi.

Subhuti! If there existed such a dharma that the Tathāgata obtained Anuttara-Samyak-Sambodhi, Dīpaṃkara Buddha would not have given his prophecy, saying, 'You will become a buddha in the coming world, and your honorific shall be "Śākyamuni."' But in reality there exists no dharma such that there is any obtaining of Anuttara-Samyak-Sambodhi.

For this reason, Dīpaṃkara Buddha gave me his prophecy and said, 'You will become a buddha in the coming world, and your honorific shall be "Śākyamuni."'

For the word 'tathāgata' means that all dharmas are just as they are without change. Some might say, 'The Tathāgata has obtained

Anuttara-Samyak-Sambodhi,' but Subhuti! In truth, there exists no dharma such that the Buddha obtains Anuttara-Samyak-Sambodhi.

Subhuti! The Anuttara-Samyak-Sambodhi obtained by Tathāgata is neither substantial nor insubstantial inside.

For this reason, the Tathāgata teaches, 'All dharmas are buddhadharma.'

Subhuti! When I speak of 'all dharmas,' these are not actually all dharmas, and so I call them by the name of 'all dharmas.'

Subhuti! It may be likened to a person having a big body."

Said Subhuti, "World Honored One! When the Tathāgata spoke of a person's body being big, this is not actually a big body, and so it is called by the name of 'big body.'"

"Subhuti! Likewise, if the bodhisattva should say, 'I have rightly delivered boundless sentient beings,' he cannot be called by the name of 'bodhisattva.'

For Subhuti! There is in reality no existence of dharma, and so he is called by the name of 'bodhisattva.' Thus the Buddha says, 'All dharma possess no self, no person, no sentient being, and no long life.'

Subhuti! If the bodhisattva says, 'I rightly cultivate the splendor of the buddha ground,' he cannot be called by the name of 'bodhisattva.'

For the cultivation of the splendor of the buddha ground spoken of by the Tathāgata is not actually cultivation of the splendor, and so it is called by the name of 'cultivation of the splendor.'

Subhuti! If the bodhisattva has mastered the dharma of selflessness, the Tathāgata will say that he is truly a bodhisattva."

Focus on

In this section, the Buddha reexamines the important content delivered thus far, summarizing it by saying that the true bodhisattva is one who masters the dharma of selflessness and puts it into practice. I hope that the reader, too, will attempt to summarize the dharma instructions up to this point and pledge to put them into practice, to consider the reasons why Dīpaṃkara Buddha uttered his words of prophecy about the Buddha, and to seek the realm that is neither substantial nor insubstantial.

Said Subhuti to the Buddha, "World Honored One! If the virtuous man and virtuous woman wish to practice the unsurpassed great Way, where are they to abide with their mind, and how are they to subdue wicked minds?"

Said the Buddha to Subhuti, "The person who aspires to the unsurpassed great Way and engages in practice must necessarily vow thus:

"He must vow to melt away the suffering of all sentient beings and lead them to enter the nirvana without residue, and he must put this into practice himself.

"He must deliver the sentient being within himself and sentient beings outside, but not fixate on the idea of having delivered sentient beings.

"For if the practitioner comes to possess the idea of having delivered sentient beings, he becomes a slave to the four misleading concepts and can never be a true bodhisattva."

The Things We Wish for Become the Course of Our Life

Here, the Buddha summarizes the things that he explained in the previous sections. He also exhorts us to engage in selflessness practice in the ultimate stage. In some sense, we can view this as a review.

The entire Way and principle of *The Diamond Sutra* is said to be contained in the word "thus." What was the Buddha's mind when he spoke? He gave two answers to two questions. First, he instructed us to make a vow. Only in so doing can things transpire according to our aspiration. A vow is a very important thing.

I once visited a temple and encountered someone who, in describing his life, said, "I suddenly found myself thinking that I needed to become a rich man someday, and that became my aspiration." One day, he went to the market and saw the merchants there earning money, and a mind surged up within him. "I also need to sell things at the market," his mind said. After that, he traveled around from market to market looking around, and he went to work selling things even before graduating from elementary school. His family tried to stop him, telling him to graduate from school, but he went to work anyway, and he was all but driven from his own home. He ultimately earned a lot of money, while his older brother and younger siblings continued on with their studies and eventually became head teachers at elementary schools.

But he said that he always experienced a sense of inferiority when comparing himself to people who had attended prestigious universities. He became curious, wondering why it was that a mind to earn money had suddenly arisen in him at that time. The family, he said, was well-off enough at the time to send him to school.

"The way I see it," I said, "is that it must have happened because you had a firm aspiration to become a rich man in a previous life, and that aspiration roared up within you like flames."

"I think you're right," he told me. The power that drives us to our destiny is the power of aspiration.

There was also a poor acquaintance of mine. This person worked to earn a doctoral degree despite suffering from terrible poverty. The poverty was truly indescribable, but this person was determined to study, and became a middle school teacher. I said that this was because of the power of aspiration—because a desire to study due to unresolved feelings about study had formed in a previous life. This person nodded and said, "I had no real desire to make any other dream come true. My only thought was of studying."

As you practice *The Diamond Sutra*, you must set the aspiration of becoming a buddha. You will be carried along by the power of aspiration even when others try to discourage you. When the Buddha tells us to set an aspiration, what he is saying is that the aspiration will lead us to awaken to the method of using our mind, that it will not let us rest until we are a buddha who delivers sentient beings.

The second answer that he gives is that we must rid ourselves of defilements and idle thoughts with a mind free of notions, and that we must use our mind with a grounding in this mind.

What makes a buddha? One becomes a buddha through proper use of the mind. Just as we cook grains into rice, happiness and misfortune in human existence are determined by the way we use our mind.

The practitioner who has resolved to achieve great, perfect, right enlightenment can never be a buddha unless he passes through these two barrier gates, and he can never avoid the suffering of samsara or escape the fetters of ignorance and desire unless he becomes a buddha. Rather than living an eternal life of torment in the burning flames of desire, the far wiser path is to engage in mind-practice toward attaining buddhahood.

How to Use the Mind

Even as we proceed toward our next life, we are unaware of its existence as we live the life of the mayfly. The misfortune that we experience was created by ourselves, but we spend our lives resenting others and blaming society.

We suffer because we do not know how to operate our mind, yet we bring that suffering upon ourselves because we have no idea how to overcome the torment, or how to pacify an angry and hateful mind. Even as we live in the universe and nature, none of us understands the principle that causes such orderly changes. Do not live this life of delusion. Resolve to become a buddha and begin engaging in profound mind-practice. This resolution is of great importance in achieving the Way of the Buddha.

The first question that Subhuti asks is where we are to abide with our mind. This is the same as asking how we should use our mind. Just as all medications have instructions that we must follow when taking them, so we will become outstanding individuals once we understand how to use the mind.

The second question is how we are to subdue wicked minds. In simple terms, Subhuti is asking how we can tame the mind. A wicked mind is one that has not been properly tamed. Who created these wicked minds? We did. We failed to tame them properly, and now they are demons that torment and gnaw at us. When we realize this and work steadily to tame them, ours will transform into the buddha mind. The person who knows how to reform his mind is one who prospers in this world. Who is it that reforms the mind? Once again, they are our own wicked minds, and we must take responsibility for reforming them.

Once you know how to fix it,
nothing in this world warrants being thrown away.
Even a dog's waste is medicine to him who knows how to use it.
Defilements and idle thoughts are merely minds
unsuited to their time and place.
How are we to carry on the mantle of history
without the desire between man and woman?

INTERPRETATION

"Subhuti! Do you believe that there is a dharma of the unsurpassed great Way that the Tathāgata obtained when he studied in the order of Dīpaṃkara Buddha?"

"There is nothing that he obtained, World Honored One! From what I gather from your teaching, you studied the Way in Dīpaṃkara Buddha's order while taking as your standard the unsurpassed great Way without any dharma by the name of 'dharma.'"

Said the Buddha, "Subhuti, the Tathāgata obtained the unsurpassed great Way that is without form.

"Subhuti! Had the Tathāgata practiced the buddhadharma while adopting as a standard and seeking to realize a dharma with form, Dīpaṃkara Buddha would not have prophesied that he would become a buddha called by the honorific 'Śākyamuni' in the next world. Because I practiced the buddhadharma while taking as my standard the dharma that possesses no fixed framework, Dīpaṃkara Buddha prophesied, 'You will become a presiding buddha by the name of Śākyamuni in the next world.'"

Dīpaṃkara Buddha's Prediction

The word *prophesied* refers to a buddha's making a prediction about what would become of someone. This means that Dīpaṃkara Buddha said that Śākyamuni Buddha would be a presiding buddha in the next world. What prompted him to predict this? He must have made this prediction about Śākyamuni Buddha after observing three aspects: the thoroughness of his belief and dedication, the thoroughness of his vow, and the certainty of the self-nature buddha as his standard in mind-practice. If the reader is certain of his belief and dedication, his vow, and his commitment to practice with the principle of the nature, the world of the gods will learn of this first and help him to attain buddhahood. It is said that when a person has made a special vow and possesses a special mind of faith, the world of the gods where the sages dwell will hold a consecration ceremony in advance to celebrate his becoming a sage.

"The word *tathāgata* means a mind that remains unchanged after experiencing all sensory conditions both with and without form. Some may say that the Buddha has obtained the unsurpassed great Way, but the truth of the tathāgata is in reality something that transcends such fixed dharmas.

The Buddha obtained that unsurpassed great Way."

The Mind That Is Just as It Is and Unchanging

The term *tathāgata* refers to someone who has obtained the mind realm without change. When we meet someone whom we find attractive, a mind of love arises in us, but that mind changes if the person does something ugly. And if that hated person does something good for us, our mind changes to one of favor.

Minds are constantly changing. Emotions are even less reliable. I remember reading a novel in which the protagonist began experiencing an uneasy mind after saying the words, "I love you." Various worries began to appear: "What will I do if that person dislikes me? What will I do if he is hurt?" These changing minds are not the mind of the tathāgata. *Tathāgata* refers to the mind when we have achieved the mind-ground that is just as it is and unchanging. This is also expressed in the words "the same mind through all dharmas."

In Korean, the word for tathāgata is *yeorae*. This consists of two Chinese characters: *yeo* (如), meaning "unchanging," and *rae* (來), meaning "to come." A mind is called tathāgata because it has an unchanging mind-ground and is just as it is when we encounter adverse conditions or favorable conditions, and when adverse and favorable conditions depart. Someone who can preserve that mind is a tathāgata. And the term "seeing the nature" refers to our understanding of this principle.

Harbored within this unchanging mind are all wisdom, all capabilities, and all minds of mercy. For this reason, the unchanging mind is also called the "perfect and complete mind." When we understand this, that is called "seeing the nature," and when we tend well to this mind, that is called "nourishing the nature." When we use that mind appropriately, that is called "commanding the nature." The person who can do all of these things well is said to have attained Anuttara-Samyak-Sambodhi. This is called "attaining buddhahood."

"Subhuti! The unsurpassed great Way realized by the Buddha is a truly peculiar realm that exists and yet does not exist, is nonexisting and yet not nonexisting.

Thus the Tathāgata has always said that among the myriad phenomena of the universe, there is none that is not the truth (buddhadharma) that is neither substantial nor insubstantial.

"Subhuti! When divided into individual entities, the myriad phenomena of the universe are all truth, and so they are not individual entities, and they are called by the name of 'the myriad phenomena of the universe.'

"Subhuti! It is like saying that a person has a big and tall body."

Said Subhuti, "World Honored One, when the Tathāgata says that a person has a big body, his words are not the big body itself but the name of 'big body.'"

If Everything Is Buddha, Where Should We Make Buddha Offerings?

We must understand that there is no phenomenon either internal or external that is not the Dharmakāya Buddha. Just as electricity flows through an electrical cord, the Dharmakāya Buddha truth flows through all the myriad phenomena of the universe. Seeing his daughter-in-law weaving hemp, Suun told a guest, "The Lord of Heaven is weaving hemp over there."

In short, he was saying that his daughter-in-law was not distinct from the Lord of Heaven.

Likewise, the Founding Master said, "Everywhere a Buddha image." Back when the Japanese were occupying Korea, a constable came by and asked where the buddha was. The Founding Master told him that if he waited a little while, the buddha would come. After a while, some members of the clergy came along on their way from farming.

Thus the mountains are water and the water mountains. The grandchild is the grandfather, and the grandfather the grandchild. In Christianity, both the grandfather and the grandson are said to call God "Father." It seems, then, that there is no generational difference in the realm of God. That place without generational differences is the realm of God, where all things are mixed together without distinction. When we mix dough, there is always moisture permeating it. In the same way, the Dharmakāya Buddha permeates the whole of this world.

The realm that is called "the Way" does not exist somewhere outside the universe. It is present in the myriad phenomena of the universe, in human society and in every last speck of dust without exception. Flowers and blades of grass are all buddhas.

I, the one delivering this lecture, am a buddha, and all of you reading my words are buddhas. All things are buddha, so what does it mean to seek the buddha? If every one of us is buddha, why is the term used only to refer to people who have achieved awakening? Consider this question.

As a proper noun, *Buddha* refers to Śākyamuni Buddha. After that, the term *buddha* is used to refer to the truth. In a word, all principles are called buddha. And the person who awakens to the buddha and puts it into practice is called a buddha.

When we use the word *truth*, we may be referring to the dharma principle concealed within the myriad phenomena of the universe, and we may be referring to what is right.

The person who views only Śākyamuni Buddha as a buddha is a novice who has yet to understand principle. Why did Śākyamuni become a buddha? It is because he awakened to the truth buddha and put it into practice. Without the truth buddha, there would have been no Śākyamuni Buddha. It was thus the existence of the truth buddha that enabled him to become Śākyamuni Buddha. When the wise practitioner respectfully honors Śākyamuni Buddha, he strives to reach his own awareness of the truth buddha that enabled Śākyamuni to become a buddha. For this reason, we should not make offerings merely to Śākyamuni Buddha when we visit a temple. We must also know to give offerings to the truth buddha harbored within all things.

The Biggest Thing Is Neither Sea Nor Sky

In expressing the greatness of his students with outstanding dharma power resulting from proper mind-practice, the Buddha likens them to Mt. Sumeru. This can be compared to the tallest mountain and greatest individual in this world. No matter what great things a person may do, there is no one leading a greater life than the life of heaven, and there is no one with greater capabilities than the person who possesses as his own the Dharmakāya Buddha that gives life to, and takes life from, the universe and all things at will. He who has unified with the Dharmakāya Buddha as something of his own is truly larger than Mt. Sumeru and great without compare to anything in this world.

We must have not a large body, but a large and broad mind. The person who regards the heaven and earth as his home and all living creatures as his family is a truly great individual. The truly great things go beyond merely the large to encompass all things large and small; they are the Il-Won Buddha and god. When we have unified with this Dharmakāya, we are great in a way that words cannot express.

"Subhuti! When bodhisattvas boast with the idea of having delivered the boundless sentient beings, they cannot be called by the name of 'bodhisattva.' For the word bodhisattva describes the practitioner who adopts the no-dharma without any traces as a standard for practice. Thus the Buddha teaches that their mind must be empty of the four misleading concepts when encountering all sensory conditions."

Repeated Urgings to Empty the Mind

A lower-level person's mind is occupied by desires. As such, he is forever using his own desires as a standard for judgment and action based on the information of what he sees and hears from outside. Before those desires melt away, his life becomes one of living under the command of desire. But after we have engaged in much cultivation of the Way, heard many dharma instructions, performed charitable services for others, and become indifferent to desires, we are then faced with the emergence of the demon that is the notion. This idea may take the form of a person's values or a sense of pride. In today's terms, it might be described as a "concept," a rule or standard that says, "The world is this or that sort of thing." It may also be a prejudice by which we declare, "Morality is this or that sort of thing." And it may be our mind of pride in having done well. Such minds form over long periods of experience and education, and they also bear a connection with the cultural climate of a particular region. The practitioner forms a concept of himself as someone with a pure mind, a kind person, a person with capabilities.

When sentient beings break free from the fetters of desire, other fetters assume a place in their mind in the form of notions. And it is the notions that accept the information that we see and hear, that consider it, make decisions, and take action, so that our lives come to revolve around those notions. Of course, desires and ideas sometimes overlap. For this reason, we cannot understand the original mind that is clear, radiant, and warm without stripping away these false notions. Nor can we possess wise judgment and unimpeded freedom. All of these things are blocked by notions and desires.

In order to eliminate notions, we must dissolve away our desires by constantly shining upon them the wisdom light of *prajñā* that appears ever numinously in the notionless original nature realm of the truth realm that is neither substantial nor insubstantial, and we must remove our notions by assessing them against the original nature.

In *The Heart Sutra*, this process of elimination with the light of the self-nature is called practice with "observing luminously." It is a process of cleansing our mind, and when our mind has long been tainted by notions and desires, we must shine the light for a long time before they go away. Desires and notions vanish straight away when assessed with sincere commitment, like the clouds clearing in the wind or snow melting in a furnace.

In this process of accepting and forming judgments about all sensory conditions with the notionless original natural realm as master, we must endeavor to make use of good notions—the mind of faith, the practicing mind, the vow, the mind of charity—and produce good discriminating minds.

We are told to abide in the mind without dwelling. The mind without dwelling is the mind that is free of notions. We are told to produce this kind of mind, and in so doing we are instructed to consider the situation and our own worthy minds when making a determination. I hope that the reader will pay heed to this explanation and clearly grasp the mind that is free of notions.

Shadows are always following us around. Eliminating them requires us to become luminous bodies. In the same way, the shadow of the false notion will naturally disappear when we develop the *prajñā* that radiates the light of our self-nature.

The city center is filled with the shadows of tall buildings.

The unskilled practitioner wears his face

powdered with pride and the mind of reputation.

How many centuries will it take

to reclaim the buddha land without notions?

Only that cloud without mind is free in nature.

INTERPRETATION

"If the bodhisattva says he has cultivated the splendor of the buddha ground, he is not yet a bodhisattva. For the Tathāgata says that the person who has cultivated the splendor of the buddha ground receives that name because he betrays no trace of the idea of having cultivated the splendor of the buddha ground.

"Subhuti! If the practitioner has awakened without obstruction to the self-nature realm that is neither occupied nor empty, then the Tathāgata will call him a true bodhisattva."

What Splendor Should We Cultivate in Our Mind?

This world is populated by individual entities, each of which bears its own characteristics. A dog and a person are both animals, but their characteristics differ. People are all people, but each of us has a unique identity. This is called the small realm of the phenomenal. But there exists something that penetrates through all these individual realms of the phenomenal. That thing is called by the names of Dharmakāya Buddha, tathāgata, and Il-Won. It is the whole—the great realm of the absolute.

This great realm is present consistently and without exception in all things. The Dharmakāya Buddha realm, this great realm, is also present within the minds of us ordinary humans and sentient beings. The thing that is referred to in *The Diamond Sutra* as "selflessness" is this great realm present within us—the realm of the tathāgata.

Ordinary humans and sentient beings are forever pushing aside the realm of selflessness and making thoughts and determinations after receiving information from the realm of the "small self," the perspective of the individual. As a result, they live in delusion and suffer the torment of a misguided existence. When we awaken to the principle of the selfless great realm and acquire training by living at all times according to the selfless mind, we will become one who has mastered the selflessness dharma for effectively harmonizing selflessness and the small self.

This section makes reference to "cultivation of splendor." The first of these cultivations consists of the cultivation of purity. This is akin to washing a bowl before making rice. No matter how well we cook rice, we cannot eat it if the bowl is dirty. For the mind to be pure, we must not have even the mind of wishing to become pure. The no-mind cultivation is the mind cultivation of buddhas. It cannot be said, however, that one achieves completion through this alone. We must cultivate on top of this the mind of charity and the mind of public well-being. And even after having done so, we must be liberated from the mind of having done so. This is the third stage of cultivation. When we have completed these three stages of cultivation—cultivation of purity, worthy cultivation with discriminating minds, and finally cultivation of freedom—we will have achieved true liberation, and the perfect and complete cultivation of the buddha and bodhisattva.

The person who has just begun devoting himself to practice focuses his energies on cultivation of purity. For the next stage, he must train himself with the cultivation of values, practicing with various skills that have value and are useful to this world.

After that, he must cultivate a freedom in which he is not bound even to those skills if he is to become an utterly perfect and great buddha who commands skills without being obstructed by them.

The practitioner who does not adopt these standards will often misunderstand things and focus solely on the first stage of purity cultivation. We need to clearly understand each stage of cultivation of splendor by buddhas, bodhisattvas, and practitioners and train ourselves accordingly.

The sentient being wanders in the darkness, obscured by clouds.
The buddha in heaven adorns the world with flower clouds.
Clouds are of a kind; what is the difference?
A wild goose approaching from the east flies off toward the south.

CHAPTER XVIII

THE FIVE DISCERNMENTS OF THE BUDDHA

Seeing All as a Single Body

He has acquired five eyes through gaining a single mind.

How many stones, how many grains of dust have gathered on the great mountain?

In a single seed, there is a flower, a leaf, a tree.

How precious, this object that bears no face.

"Subhuti! What do you think?
Does the Tathāgata possess the physical eye?"

"Yes, World Honored One.
The Tathāgata possesses the physical eye."

"Subhuti! What do you think?
Does the Tathāgata possess the divine eye?"

"Yes, World Honored One.
The Tathāgata possesses the divine eye."

"Subhuti! What do you think?
Does the Tathāgata possess the wisdom eye?"

"Yes, World Honored One.
The Tathāgata possesses the wisdom eye."

"Subhuti! What do you think?
Does the Tathāgata possess the dharma eye?"

"Yes, World Honored One.
The Tathāgata possesses the dharma eye."

"Subhuti! What do you think?
Does the Tathāgata possess the buddha eye?"

"Yes, World Honored One.
The Tathāgata possesses the buddha eye."

"Subhuti! What do you think? Has the Buddha made analogies to the grains of sand in the Ganges River in his teachings?"

"He has, World Honored One. The Tathāgata has spoken of this sand."

"Subhuti! What do you think? Were there were as many Ganges Rivers as there are grains of sand in a single Ganges River, and were there as many buddha worlds as those grains of sand in all those Ganges Rivers, this would be a great number, would it not?"

"Truly great, World Honored One!"

Said the Buddha to Subhuti, "The Tathāgata knows all the different minds of all the sentient beings in this land.

For all the minds spoken of by the Tathāgata are not minds, and so they are called by the name of 'minds.'

For Subhuti! If the mind of the past cannot be obtained, neither than the mind of the present be obtained, nor can the mind of the future be obtained."

Focus on

This section explains how the buddha possesses five eyes, giving him the wisdom to completely understand the different minds of sentient beings. Here, we will examine the kind of practice that we must perform to develop the same eyes, and we will learn about and analyze each of them.

"Subhuti! Do you believe the Tathāgata possesses the physical eye, the divine eye, the wisdom eye, the dharma eye, and the buddha eye?"

Said Subhuti, "He has all of these: the physical eye, the divine eye, the wisdom eye, the dharma eye, and the buddha eye."

Opening Our Mind's Eye

The physical eye is the one that is part of our body. The divine eye can clearly see even those things that are not visible to the physical eye, a phenomenon that the Founding Master called "numinous penetration." Those who engage in much cultivation are said to gain a clearer spirit, allowing them to understand the minds of others as though seeing them reflected in a mirror.

The "wisdom eye" refers to the ability to estimate things based on the principles gained through much Inquiry into Human Affairs and Universal Principles. It is a condition in which we have a clear understanding of the realm of the nature and the principle of retribution and response of cause and effect. Ultimately, the divine eye and the wisdom eye are one and the same, but the former is developed when we focus on clearing our spirit, and the latter is attained when we devote ourselves to Inquiry into Human Affairs and Universal Principles.

With the divine eye, we achieve numinous penetration and understand the things reflected in our mind mirror after we have engaged in much cultivation, even though we may not have awakened to the Way. The wisdom eye can only be attained through study of the scriptures and cases for questioning. When we do so, we see the nature, and our perception becomes radiant. This is called "penetration of the Way."

The dharma eye, also called "penetration of dharma," comes when we perform much practice with Choice in Action. It refers to our gaining a clear understanding with our affairs—the realization of "This is how such-and-such affair should be handled." When the buddha encounters some situation, he understands the proper sequence for dealing with it. In formulating a dharma, we must have penetration of dharma. In the past, rules of propriety were crafted in which there was discrimination between men and women. In the age to come, however, there will be no such discrimination, and so we must formulate rules of propriety that do not discriminate between men and women. Doing so will require our achieving penetration of dharma and gaining the dharma eye. This eye only emerges when a person is an enlightened one above the status of "Beyond the Household."

When we consult with senior practitioners, they always present us with methods. Sometimes, it seems that the methods are not suited to our ideas, but when we try them they turn out to be correct. If the wisdom eye means our eyes are open to principles, then the dharma eye refers to the ability to handle affairs at the level of phenomena.

The buddha eye is the eye of mercy possessed by the buddha, his ability to examine a sentient being's spiritual capacity and soothe the part that itches or aches, to comfort him and share the suffering. This buddha eye is what we gain through the combination of the aforementioned divine eye, wisdom eye, and dharma eye.

After achieving great enlightenment, the Founding Master is supposed to have said, "I wish someone would ask what I do not know." He expressed dismay that, having suffered from ignorance in the past, he had no one whom he could tell about what he came to understand after achieving enlightenment. When we achieve great enlightenment and right enlightenment, we gain all five eyes at once.

The ordinary person possesses only the physical eye. Depending on the buddha's knowledge and perspective and the practitioner's abilities, however, some may possess the wisdom eye, others the dharma eye, and still others the divine eye. Out of all of these, the wisdom eye is the most important, the one that should be possessed first. The proper sequence is observed when we first see the nature and gain a clear understanding of the principle of cause and effect, and then achieve penetration of the Way and the other forms of penetration.

The Buddha is said to have possessed the five eyes, but we, too, harbor within us the necessary elements to possess them. We simply have not cultivated them. I have an audio system in my room, but I only use one or two of the features; I have no idea how to use the rest. People ask me, "Why don't you use this feature? Why do you only listen to this kind of thing?" No matter how many features an audio system has, they are useless if we do not know how to use them. Likewise, we sentient beings have in our realm of self-nature all the abilities to possess the five eyes, but we leave them unused and merely employ the worst of them, the physical eye. In the Buddha's eyes, sentient beings can only appear genuinely foolish. Let us also make a vow to develop the jewels hidden within our ourselves and become buddhas possessing the five eyes.

Downtown Seoul is nothing but haste and hasty people.
Closer examination reveals that it need not be done.
Sentient beings are anxiously chasing their desires.
Ignorant of the Way,
the practitioner is anxious with minor practice.
We cannot fathom what the buddha
without desires busies himself with.

"Subhuti! Did the Buddha speak about the grains of sand in the Ganges?"

"He did. The Buddha made many analogies to the grains of sand in the Ganges in his explanation."

"Subhuti! Were there were as many Ganges Rivers as there are grains of sand in a single Ganges, the number of all the grains of sand in all those Ganges Rivers would be truly great, would it not? And if there were as many buddha worlds as those grains of sand, that, too, would be a great number, would it not?"

"Truly great, World Honored One!"

Said the Buddha to Subhuti, "The Tathāgata knows all the different minds of all the sentient beings in this land. This is so because all those sentient being minds of which I have just spoken are not true minds, and so the word 'mind' is a name applied to them."

The Insight of the Buddha

The Buddha achieved great, perfect, right enlightenment through proper use of the light of wisdom harbored within his mind. Not only did he understand all of his own mind worlds, but he also possessed the great wisdom to understand all the principles and phenomena of this world.

The Founding Master said that this world consists of three structures.

First, there are all the individual entities that make up the myriad phenomena of the universe. There exists a principle that governs all of these things. It is called the great realm of the absolute because it runs through all things and governs over them.

Second, there are the distinctive characteristics possessed by all individual things. For instance, people are all the same in being people, but we can classify different people as impatient or slow. There exists a principle, however, such that each individual can only be that way. This is called the small realm of the phenomenal.

Third, these individuals do not simply stand still. All of them are in a constant process of change. Places and shapes and colors—all of them are undergoing change. This is called the realm of being and nonbeing, meaning that they are changing through emergence and disappearance.

The Buddha says that he knows all about the great realm of the absolute and the small realm of individual phenomena, how these things are changing and what they are becoming.

Imagine as many Ganges Rivers as there are grains of sand in the Ganges. How truly vast a number of grains of sand there would be in all those rivers. Such a boundless number of entities makes up this universe. And there is a principle that runs through all of them. When we awaken for certain and understand that principle, it is said, we will understand the nature and essence of all individual things.

Each of the individual things in this universe has its own distinctive characteristics. When we classify these characteristics, we will find *yin* and *yang*, cause and effect. We can divide them further to find the Eight Symbols from the *Book of Changes*, and still further to isolate the 64 trigrams. The changing and motion of those individuals over time is described as the realm of being and nonbeing, and as transformation. The Buddha understood the principle behind all the individual objects as numerous as the grains of sand in the Ganges, the principle by which they all return to one thing despite their different names, and so he is said to have achieved great enlightenment and the thousand enlightenments and ten thousand penetrations. The myriad dharmas returned to one thing. Where is that realm where all things returned to one? And where will the one thing to which all things return itself return to? Let us examine this.

"Subhuti! The mind in which the buddha abides is a truly mysterious and marvelous mind that could not be obtained in the past and cannot be obtained in the present, nor can it be obtained in the future."

Obtaining the Mind That Cannot Be Obtained

The Buddha speaks here of the realm of a mind that could not be obtained in the past, cannot be obtained in the present, and cannot be obtained in the future. That mind realm is one that cannot be obtained, nor can it be put into words.

A Zen monk named Cijue gave the following dharma instruction:

"Before the buddhas of antiquity appeared

This one shape was perfectly round.

...even Śākyamuni could not comprehend it.

How could Mahākāśyapa transmit it?"

The realm cannot be understood, and thus it cannot be obtained. Furthermore, because it cannot be obtained, it cannot be explained. Because of this, it is a mind that could not be obtained in the past and cannot be obtained in the present and future. We speak of the tortuous experience that Koreans endured under the harsh rule of the Japanese. We also speak readily of our enjoyable experiences. In this way, the discriminating mind capably recollects and speaks accordingly. But the original mind is one that cannot be obtained. From what you have learned of *The Diamond Sutra* thus far, you may be able to gather something of this mind that cannot be obtained.

There is one story that cannot be omitted when studying this chapter. Long ago, there was a man named "Diamond" Zhou (he later came to be known as Zen Master Deshan). He was extremely fond of *The Diamond Sutra* and studied it a great deal. He is said to have understood it thoroughly and to have interpreted it very well.

At the time, there was a famous monk in the south by the name of Longtan. Longtan had not studied *The Diamond Sutra* very much, but he was said to have a very clear understanding of it. Learning of this, Zhou rolled up a copy of the Sutra and headed south. He went to a restaurant near the entrance of Longtan's temple to eat lunch. In Korean, the word for lunch is *jeomsim*, which combines the character *jeom* (點) meaning "mark" and the character *sim* (心) meaning "mind." When Zhou asked for his lunch, the old woman at the restaurant looked at what he was carrying and asked him what kind of text it was. He told her that it was *The Diamond Sutra*, and she asked him if he knew much about the Sutra. He responded that he had been studying it for decades and knew every word of it. Hearing this, the woman said:

"The past mind cannot be obtained, the present mind cannot be obtained, and the future mind cannot be obtained. Which mind will you be marking to eat your lunch?"

Zhou was at a loss, unable to give an answer. It is said that he went on his way to Longtan's temple without being able to obtain a meal.

Later, Zhou met Longtan and saw the nature. For all his reading, he had been unable to do so, yet he saw the nature from hearing a single dharma instruction from a teacher.

For there is a principle whereby you eat your meal and I belch.

Our sickness is cured after a deep sleep.

It is easy, very easy; there is nothing easier.

Standing tall on Mt. Byeonsan,

the rock listens to the sound of a stream.

CHAPTER XIX

THE MERITS OF GIVING THE SEVEN TREASURES
Edifying on the Entire Dharma Realm

A mountain of the seven treasures fills the heaven and earth.
Who will understand the message of "it is not so" and "cast it aside"?
On the day we tear apart the void
There will be not one thing in heaven, earth, and nature to cast aside.

"Subhuti! What do you think?

If someone performs charitable service with enough of the seven treasures to fill the Three Thousand Great Thousand Worlds, will the person gain many blessings through these causes and conditions?"

"Yes, World Honored One! The person will receive a great many blessings through these causes and conditions."

"Subhuti! If the blessings and merits had a true image, the Tathāgata would not say that many blessings and merits are obtained, but because there are no blessings and merits, the Tathāgata says that there are many blessings and merits."

Focus on

This section teaches that while charitable offerings with the seven treasures may be great in size and in number, they are limited and cannot offer true happiness. I hope that you will seriously consider why it is mistaken to attempt to gain happiness as sentient beings do, through possessing things with form, and make the effort to correct the course of the mind's pursuits.

"Subhuti! If someone performs charitable service with enough of the seven treasures to fill the universe, will he gain many blessings through these causes and conditions?"

"Yes, World Honored One!

He will receive a great many blessings."

"Subhuti! If the blessings of the seven treasures made a human being sincerely happy, I would not have expressed them in terms of number. But the blessings of the seven treasures cannot deliver true happiness, nor can one become a tathāgata with many blessings.

I merely used a relative expression in saying the blessings are many."

Do Not Be Taken In by Blessings and Happiness

When we perform many charitable acts with material things, the rewards come to us in the form of a multitude of blessings. But while we may enjoy many blessings externally, they do not guarantee human happiness. Blessings are good when a person receives them well and commands them well, but when he does so poorly, disaster is sure to follow the blessings, and the mind of conceit will follow. Moreover, he will fail to understand that this is karma from previous lives, and he will come to believe that blessings are ever present, with the result that he despises those who are not blessed. In addition to this negative aspect that arises as a result of blessings, we also come to exert many efforts to preserve our blessings, so that desire arises and we suffer torment in our mind.

I once asked myself whether I was living to manage objects or whether objects existed for my sake. There are probably more instances where we are a slave to our possessions. Thus it is said in Buddhism, "When an object appears, so does a defilement."

Blessings that come from outside become a snare that prevents us from being free. They torment our minds and make us lazy and uneasy. For this reason, we must find and cultivate the source of blessings that lies harbored within our mind. If we acquire training with proper use of our mind and we gain material blessings in addition to that, then it is icing on the cake.

We must not be taken in by blessings. We must avoid being manipulated by objects or honors. When we are, desire emerges, torments build up, and we come to hate others and finally to cycle in samsara. Samsara is a truly fearsome punishment. Right now, we may be enjoying blessings with the human body that we have received. But when this body dies and our soul moves on to the next life, our life of being the pawn of material things will result in the selection of a next life with a darkened mind. We may receive our karma through proceeding into the body of a beast, or through not receiving any body at all and roaming the world of ghosts.

If we interpret the Buddha's words as saying that the merits from performing various charitable acts are a bad thing, then we have misunderstood them. What he says is that we must not spend our life solely pursuing material values. In order to gain freedom of the mind, we need to practice cultivation of the Way in addition to our material life. In other words, what the Buddha is ultimately calling for, the form of the ideal person, is one who can achieve a harmony between a material life and a spiritual life, where he uses material things all the more after gaining freedom of the mind.

> Bad habits are the seeds of wickedness,
> good habits the seeds of virtue.
> Seeds of wickedness summon punishment,
> seeds of good bring blessings.
> The wicked one suffers torturous pain,
> the virtuous one great pleasure,
> And the tathāgata is merry amid good and evil
> and the winds of the eight kinds of sensory conditions.

CHAPTER XX

THE UNKNOWABLE MIND OF THE BUDDHA

Leaving Both Form and Appearance

Seen yet unseeable, heard yet unhearable.

We long and long to see our circular one,

Seeming to go, seeming to come, yet always the same face.

We greet it in the morning and evening, and walk with it all day long.

"Subhuti! What do you think? Can one recognize the Buddha from his perfectly endowed appearance?"

"No, World Honored One. One cannot recognize the Tathāgata from his perfectly endowed appearance.

For the perfectly endowed appearance spoken of by the Tathāgata is not a perfectly endowed appearance, and thus is called by the name of 'perfectly endowed appearance.'"

"Subhuti! What do you think? Can one recognize the Buddha Tathāgata from his being perfectly endowed with appearances?"

"No, World Honored One. One cannot recognize the Tathāgata from his being perfectly endowed with appearances. For the 'being perfectly endowed with appearances' spoken of by the Tathāgata is not a perfect endowment, and thus is called by the name of 'being perfectly endowed with appearances.'"

Focus on

This section teaches that the Tathāgata is one who cannot be understood in terms of forms or knowledge alone. Here, we will need to study how we ought not to fixate on appearance when gauging the character of the buddha, and how one is not a buddha simply because he possesses vast knowledge and a good heart.

"Subhuti! Can it be said that someone is a buddha simply because he is endowed with an attractive appearance in every respect?"

"No, World Honored One! No matter how handsome or flawlessly attractive one may be, one cannot believe that he is a buddha. For the faultless body of which you have just spoken is not eternally perfect, and buddhahood does not reside in the attractiveness or humbleness of his body."

Seek Not Elsewhere But in the Mind

We have no way of knowing how physically attractive the Buddha was, but it seems that he gave this particular dharma instruction many times because of all the people at the time who misunderstood and said, "I think he must be a buddha—look at how beautiful he is!" He says these words repeatedly. It is said that 32 basic terms were used to describe the Buddha's attractiveness, and as many as 80 specific terms. When sentient beings fixated on his physical beauty, he instructed them to let go of that fixation.

No matter how attractive we make our bodies, all of us will end up as corpses. We are sacks of blood and water. Of this, Venerable Bojo said, "Let go of your sack of flesh!" His message is that we are unable to engage in great practice because of our fixation on the flesh. If we invested into mind-practice even half the commitment that we give to our bodies, it is said we would immediately see the nature and achieve buddhahood. It is not the case, however, that we should treat our body recklessly. If we do, the buddha within cannot lead a wholesome life. We must therefore minister well to our body, but at the same time avoid simply accommodating its desires.

Back during Korea's Yi Dynasty, a loyal subject by the name of Sŏng Sam-mun sang these words as he was being dragged off to his execution:

"The drum rings out and calls for my life.

I raise my head and see the sun beginning to set in the west.

It is said there are no inns on the way to the afterlife.

Where am I to sleep this evening?"

If we look at the words of this song, we will see that they are what the faithful Sŏng Sam-mun, one of the Six Martyred Ministers, sang in his worry about his imminent death. After we die, our body is nothing more than an inn. Where do we go once we leave those lodgings? Let us not fixate on the body, but control it well and avoid becoming the practitioner who fails to attain buddhahood as a result of his body.

The person whose mind is governed by the flesh is a sentient being. The person whose body is governed by the mind is a practitioner of the Way. And when we hone and use blessings and wisdom, creating a proper harmony between spirit and body, we become buddhas.

As something possessing form, the body is false, even when it is a buddha's body. We must not seek buddha in the body, but worship and revere the Dharmakāya concealed in the mind within the body, and devote ourselves to cultivating the Way so that we use it without ever losing sight of this.

INTERPRETATION

"Subhuti! Can it be said that someone is a tathāgata because he has a kind heart and abundant knowledge?"

"It cannot. The word *tathāgata* does not describe someone who possesses a kind heart and abundant knowledge. For even when someone possesses all of the good methods of mind use and knowledge that you have described, he cannot be called complete if he is obscured by notions. One can only be called tathāgata when he has realized the realm that is neither substantial nor insubstantial."

The Minds Exchanged by Buddhabodhisattvas

We have minds to perform charitable service for others and offer charitable gifts. Such minds are truly good. It is also good to be very learned in a wide range of fields. But even if someone possesses abundant knowledge, a kind heart, and many talents, he cannot be said to be tathāgata because of this, for *tathāgata* refers to the foundation realm from which all minds emerge.

There was a *Won*-Buddhist who said that he wanted to leave a fortune to his son, but that he was unable to instill a mind of diligence in him. I told him, "Really, you don't have to leave him money. But the best approach would be to communicate the mind of diligence to your child, for one becomes rich with a mind of diligence, economy, and charity to others."

What mind would the buddha communicate to his students? The buddha would convey the foundational realm from which the diligent mind, charitable mind, and economizing mind all emerge. It cannot be said, then, that someone is a tathāgata even if he possesses a good heart and abundant knowledge, for the tathāgata is the realm from which all things issue forth.

The parents who pass on only material things to their children will hear those children say, "Our parents are ordinary people."

The parents who pass on minds of loyalty to one's country and diligence will be called righteous and patriotic by their children, while those who pass on the perfect and complete, utterly impartial and unselfish mind will hear their children say, "Our parents are buddhas and bodhisattvas." This is why Confucius said that "the superior person is not a vessel." It is because he is not fixed like a vessel. The gentleman is someone who studies the realm of the tathāgata.

> Ordinary people give their children the deed to the house.
> Righteous people show a righteous mind to all the world.
> Śākyamuni Buddha and Mahākāśyapa
> Exchanged the heaven and earth without masters.
> This is no secret, but something well known to him
> who is able to know.

CHAPTER XXI

WORDS THAT CANNOT BE EXPRESSED IN WORDS

No Speaking and Nothing Spoken

No path exists in all the heavens and earth,

yet it clearly comes and goes along a path.

By its nature, it is twisted when spoken,

yet it opens up with the word.

We must simply beware of failing to understand

the gold vein within the stone.

What mind are you marking right now?

"Subhuti! Do not say that the Tathāgata believes, 'There exists a dharma that I have properly taught.'

"Do not entertain this thought. For if a person should say, 'There exists a dharma that the Tathāgata has taught,' this is a slander against the Buddha. For he has failed to understand my teachings.

"Subhuti! 'Dharma discourse' is merely a name, as no dharma exists to be taught."

At this time, the wise [Ayusmant] Subhuti said to the Buddha, "World Honored One! Will sentient beings exist in the world of the future to hear the teaching of this dharma and produce minds of belief?"

Said the Buddha, "Subhuti! They are not sentient beings, nor are they not sentient beings. For Subhuti! The Tathāgata says that they are not sentient beings, and merely calls them by the name of 'sentient beings.'"

Focus on

In this chapter, the Buddha shows that we need a clear understanding of the purpose of using words to teach the dharma that cannot be expressed in words. The truth is a realm that can never be fully expressed in language and writing, but it has been rendered into language for the ultimate purpose of teaching sentient beings. I therefore hope that you will commit yourselves sincerely to understanding the content that is taught through language.

"Subhuti! You should not say that the Tathāgata believes that he has taught the dharma. For if anyone says that the Tathāgata has taught the dharma, this is a slander on the Buddha. And it can therefore be said that this person does not properly understand the original intent of what is taught.

"Subhuti! In teaching the dharma, one is forced to explain as a dharma a realm that cannot be given form, and so the name of 'dharma discourse' is given."

Only the Mind

In the Il-Won-Sang Vow, the Founding Master described the Il-Won-Sang Truth as a tranquil realm of samādhi beyond all words and speech, a realm that transcends being and nonbeing. This Il-Won-Sang realm is the same Dharmakāya Buddha realm and tathāgata realm of which the Buddha seeks to teach us. Such a realm is utterly beyond the power of words to express, and when the Dharmakāya Buddha realm is expressed in words, it is already not that realm.

The Buddha teaches of the dharma of no-action disconnected from the path of language: when disciples say that he has taught that realm, they have failed to understand the Buddha's true intent. Furthermore, they are ultimately saying that the Buddha has taught a dharma of action in which teachings are present, even though the Buddha taught a dharma of no-action. The result is thus a slandering and demotion of the Buddha.

How many students are there in this world who have a proper understanding of their teacher's intentions? If they understood even 60 percent of their teacher's intentions and worked to put them into practice, ours would be a world of peace, and morality would have enjoyed a revival. Just as there are few children who understand their parents' minds, so we find here a practical concern among sages with regard to religion.

Recently, I heard someone say, after hearing *The Diamond Sutra*, that they had a flickering understanding of that realm. "What exists to make it seem understood and yet not understood?"

It has been said that the Way does not belong among those things that can be understood or not understood. The realm is the same for both the person who understands and the person who fails to understand. After awakening to the Way, Venerable Huineng ended up running away, wandering the south for over a decade before finally arriving at a temple. The head monk there was Renzong. A group of monks were having a debate when a wind suddenly started up and a flag began to flutter.

"Look!" cried one of the monks. "The flag is moving!"

"What do you mean?" said the monk next to him. "How can a flag move by itself? The wind is moving the flag!"

And so the monks split into two groups: a "moving flag" group arguing that the flag moved regardless of the wind, and a "moving wind" group arguing that the flag's movement was caused by the wind.

Seeing this, Huineng said, "The cause is the movement of the mind. Is it not your minds that are moving?"

He proceeded to deliver a dharma instruction. "You sense that the flag is moving because your minds are moving," he told them. It is said that the monks then realized that Huineng was a great man and began to study under him.

When we believe that the flag is moving, we are describing the "phenomenon" as it is. And when we say that it moves because of the wind, we are thinking of its "cause."

What kind of effect does it have on our life, and human life, when we say that the flag is moving by itself or due to the wind? Ultimately, we can see something as positive or negative depending on how our minds operate as we observe the phenomenon. The operation of our mind is the most important thing as we live our life. What would have happened in that situation if their minds had not moved? How would we characterize that moment? That kind of realm, where you hear my words but do not move, is called tathāgata. However, we must not fixate on this word, either.

What if the flag is moving? And what if it is the wind that moves?

In a sea of minds, human life is lived according to the mind.

He who says "little" when there is much,

he who says "much" when there is little,

Creates billions of joys and torments with ten thousand minds.

Do you understand? I understand. It is only the mind.

INTERPRETATION

At this time, the wise Subhuti said to the Buddha, "Will those sentient beings produce true minds of faith after hearing the teachings of this the Buddha's *Diamond Sutra* in the future world?"

Said the Buddha, "Subhuti! Those sentient beings are not sentient beings, for they all harbor self-nature buddhas within. They may be called by the name of 'sentient beings' because they fail to put their self-nature buddha into practice. But while the Tathāgata thinks of sentient beings as buddhas, people give them the name of 'sentient beings,' and so I refer to them in that way."

Let Us Use Our Mind Well

What we should understand from this passage is the Buddha's perspective in viewing sentient beings. He does not bind sentient beings with a definition as sentient beings, since they harbor the same buddha nature that he does. He merely uses the name "sentient beings" as a term to distinguish them from buddhas. In a similar way, because they have not cultivated their buddha nature and put it into practice, they therefore cannot be called buddhas.

When we visit gold-mining regions, we find gold ore. This is in fact stone, but it is described as gold ore because there is gold inside of that stone. We cannot say that it is entirely gold, because the gold and rock have not been separated out, but it is called by the name of "gold ore" as a way of distinguishing gold and stone. We can understand the Buddha's message along the same lines.

Computers have become very widespread in recent years. It has been said that only the very expert use all of the features available on them. As for ordinary people, there are those who use only the word-processing features, though with a bit of effort they are able to use other features. And when they put even more specialized effort into teaching themselves, they can learn to use everything.

Our minds carry within them the pure liberation mind possessed by the buddha, the myriad wisdoms, and the greatly compassionate mind of mercy. The mind is the most precious treasure, yet sentient beings misuse that mind to commit transgressions. The thief uses his mind to steal and the swindler uses it to deceive others, while the kind person uses it for kindness, the scholar uses it to acquire knowledge, and the artist uses it to create images.

Let us focus our efforts on awakening the mind principle of which the Buddha spoke, training it well and using that mind in our interactions with the community, so that we achieve buddhahood.

We cook the grains or knead them into cakes, but all is rice.
The stone buddha and stone lion are both stone.
Though their aspect and application may differ, all are of a kind.
The myriad kinds are one, and the one, myriad kinds.

CHAPTER XXII

THE UNATTAINABLE MIND

No Dharma That Can Be Attained

We wash away all manner of grime with water.
What must we use to cleanse the grime from the water?
We scrub and scrub, yet it does not wash away.
Illuminate the realm that can be neither grasped nor released.

Said Subhuti to the Buddha, "World Honored One! In attaining the Anuttara-Samyak-Sambodhi, did the Buddha attain nothing?"

Said the Buddha, "Yes, it is just so.

"Subhuti! I did not obtain even the smallest dharma in the Anuttara-Samyak-Sambodhi, and I thus call it by the name of 'Anuttara-Samyak-Sambodhi.'"

Focus on

In this passage, the Buddha explains that the goal and ultimate state of Buddhism is realization of the unattainable mind realm. By its nature, the mind is something that does not disappear even when released, and that is not held even when grasped. This realm exists equally in everyone. I hope that the reader of this chapter will practice toward becoming a truly fine individual who possesses the unattainable realm.

Said Subhuti to the Buddha, "Is there no trace of your having attained the unsurpassed great Way that you have realized?"

Said the Buddha, "Yes, it is so. Subhuti! My unsurpassed great Way is such a realm that one cannot find even the very smallest trace. This dharma I call by the name of 'unsurpassed great Way.'"

Wipe the Grime from the Mirror

I recall the lyrics of a song from long ago. In it, Yang Guifei, the great Chinese beauty, calls out to her servant Little Jade. She is not summoning Little Jade to do something for her. Rather, she is calling her handmaiden simply because she wants her beloved An Lushan to know that she is waiting outside.

The same is true for study of *The Diamond Sutra*. We study it to see and know the tathāgata realm within our mind. We need to look into the mirror of *The Diamond Sutra* and see our own mind reflected in it. For this reason, we and *The Diamond Sutra* must exist together.

There was a monk named Xiangyan who lived with and served another monk named Weishan. Looking at Xiangyan, Weishan asked him, "What did you look like before you were born from your parents?

And what kind of mind exists before a single thought emerges?"

Xiangyan searched through the sutras for an answer, but there was none to be found. So he burned them all and wandered about with a resigned mind. One day, he was cleaning up in the temple of the State Preceptor, Huizhong of the South. As he was sweeping, the broom struck a stone, which bounced off a bamboo tree with a "crack." At that moment, he experienced awakening. After hearing that "crack," he awakened to the fact that the original realm is a realm that, by its nature, cannot be expressed in words.

Xiangyan experienced this kind of awakening by happenstance because he was someone who was ordinarily very attentive and concerned about the truth. People who typically lack attentiveness do not recognize what they are clutching in their hands. The Founding Master said that questioning is the key to great enlightenment. Only through our harboring questions about the principle of the nature does awakening occur. Countries and companies only prosper when there is an awareness of problem areas. We must work tenaciously to discover problems and solve them.

> Pauper! The door to paradise will open.
> Greatly blessed one! The door to hell awaits.
> See precisely which of the two doorways you are heading for.
> The Tathāgata dwells where there are no doors.
> Do you understand?

CHAPTER XXIII

THE MIND THAT WE ALL POSSESS EQUALLY

Doing Good with a Pure Mind

The mountains are the water, the water is the mountains.

This is the eye of the peak of Mt. Sumeru.

The mountains are mountains, the water is water.

This is the eyebrow of the ten million enlightened masters.

"And Subhuti! This dharma is equal, without high or low, and it is thus called by the name of 'Anuttara-Samyak-Sambodhi.'

"One who cultivates all wholesome dharma without the self, without the person, without the sentient being, and without long life will achieve Anuttara-Samyak-Sambodhi.

"Subhuti! When I speak of 'wholesome dharmas,' the Tathāgata has explained that these are not wholesome dharmas, and so he uses the name of 'wholesome dharmas.'"

Focus on

We realize the unsurpassed great Way when we perform all acts of good based in the equality dharma that is devoid of the four misleading concepts. The practitioner can attain the mind of equality when he rids himself of desire, as well as higher-level fixed ideas. It is only when we are grounded in this mind of equality that we develop the ability to use the right mind for the sensory conditions that we encounter. I hope that the reader will seek the mind of equality, and thereby inquire into the true wisdom suited to all things.

"Subhuti! This no-dharma is equal, a truth present in all objects without distinctions of high or low, and it is called by the name of 'unsurpassed great Way.' It can therefore be said that one is realizing the perfect unsurpassed great Way when one has been instilled with the mind free of the four notions so that grace extends to all sensory conditions.

"Subhuti! My dharma of which I spoke before is neither bound in notions nor fixed, and it is therefore called by the name of 'most outstanding dharma.'"

The Dharmakāya Buddha That Is No More Present in Buddhas or Less Present in Sentient Beings

The truth revealed by the Buddha, the unsurpassed great Way that he has explained thus far, is harbored equally within all things. The Il-Won-Sang Truth is not present more in the buddha because he is outstanding, nor is it present less simply because one is an ordinary human or sentient being. The truth is that which exists equally and identically in buddhas and sentient beings.

Here, the Buddha describes two methods of training for when we have awakened to the fact that the truth-realm of the tathāgata is equal. One involves constant effort to recover the realm without notions in our mind. This means working at all times to restore the realm devoid of the four misleading concepts.

If we view this in terms of stages, the first involves recovering that realm when a desire arises, and thereby dissolving that desire. Once we have rid ourselves of desires, however, we are susceptible to the emergence of the self notion, the idea of our having achieved awakening. We must train ourselves with practice to eliminate concepts such as the concept of a self, the concept of a person, the concept of a sentient being, or the concept of a long life when they arise. When we have rid ourselves of the four misleading concepts, we must also discipline ourselves with all wholesome dharmas. And while we are disciplining ourselves well with the realm devoid of the four concepts, or signs, our process of becoming buddhas consists of disciplining all the wholesome dharmas—the mind of faith through which we respect our teacher, as well as public spirit—along with practice so that one who does not know how to study becomes one who studies well, practice so that one who does not know how to teach becomes one who teaches well, practice with the life of gratitude, and practice with the life of self-power.

After we have cultivated the endless dharmas with the dharma of no-action, we must discipline the various discriminating minds that we possess. In answer to the question of what we need to do after achieving the state in which we do not abide anywhere even while responding, we should practice with charitable giving as appropriate for specific times and places. Cultivating all virtues means performing charitable service.

When we practice incorrectly, we regard abiding with the mind in the place without dwelling as the only thing of importance, and we view doing so as the only method of practice. What we should do to make the mind pure is to make wise decisions as we encounter situations. In so doing, we are making preparations to enjoy many blessings in our real life and to create charitable merits for society and our neighbors. We must understand for certain that perfect practice means adopting as our foundation the instilling of the pure mind without dwelling, and knowing how to focus our efforts on manifesting charitable merits.

> Of all things in this world, there is none that is not Dharmakāya.
> Buddhas and sentient beings are utterly equal.
> Where, then, are you to make buddha offerings
> as you ask for blessings?
> When thirsty, you should drink water; when longing,
> look at the moon and weep.

CHAPTER XXIV

THE INCOMPARABLE MERIT

Blessings and Wisdom Without Compare

The sky for the frog in the well, the void for the roc.

They are merely the same thing; what is the difference?

Are they not different only in where they lie?

The white snow swirls in the void, and I am here.

"Subhuti! Even if one were to perform charitable service for others with a mountain of the seven treasures the size of all the King Mt. Sumerus in the Three Thousand Great Thousand Worlds, the merits would not be even one-hundredth those of another person who accepts and upholds, reads and recites, and teaches others the four-line gathas with this *Prajna-Paramita Sūtra*, nor could they be likened to even one-hundredth of one-thousandth of one ten-thousandth of one hundred-millionth, or any number."

Focus on

In this section, we are taught that the merit of accepting and holding, and reading and reciting, *The Diamond Sutra* is great without compare. We must distinguish clearly that which we should do before all else, and we must dedicate even greater commitment to that. The merits of the world are all relative, and all are extinguished in the end. The mind-practice taught by the Buddha is absolute and never extinguished. I hope that you will commit yourself more sincerely to absolute merits.

The Merits of Teaching the Diamond Mind

As described before, the greatest merit in the world is that of studying *The Diamond Sutra*, putting it into practice, and teaching it to others. Practicing *The Diamond Sutra* means using the mind that is like the void. We must grab hold of the realm without fixation in our mind, the mind that transcends all things, and swallow the core of *The Diamond Sutra*. We must not allow our practice of *The Diamond Sutra* to be separate from ourselves. We must seize the standard and declare, "*The Diamond Sutra* instructs me to use the mind without notions!"

I recall back when I was serving under a certain dharma teacher. During that time, I asked this teacher to lecture on *The Diamond Sutra*. The teacher told me that I was foolish, that he was always lecturing on *The Diamond Sutra*. I asked him when he had taught it, and he merely said that he was always doing so. Hearing this, I thought that it was truly marvelous. Once someone has consumed *The Diamond Sutra*, he reveals *The Diamond Sutra* in its entirety wherever he happens to be. Such a person controls *The Diamond Sutra* wherever he goes, while the person who has not done so is controlled by *The Diamond Sutra* wherever he goes. We can practice *The Diamond Sutra* day and night, only to end up merely becoming its slave. If we can go through our life commanding *The Diamond Sutra*, we become ones who act and teach *The Diamond Sutra*.

Those who perform many acts of charity without any knowledge of *The Diamond Sutra* truth will see their wisdom darkened as a result of the blessings that arise from those charitable acts. This becomes the cause of resentment toward others and laziness in themselves. But for those who receive and uphold, read and recite *The Diamond Sutra*, who put it into practice by using their mind well like a buddha, and who teach it to others and guide them to practice it, the merits are greater than any in this world.

The Founding Master, too, said that the greatest merit of all is that of communicating to others the truth that neither arises nor ceases and the principle of retribution and response of cause and effect. The principle of retribution and response of cause and effect and the principle that neither arises nor ceases is none other than *The Diamond Sutra*.

Can we be happy if our mind is tormented, even if we are rich? The settled mind is the ultimate bliss. When we have a settled mind, we experience ultimate bliss even if we have no money. The person who enjoys great honors, commands great knowledge, and possesses a great fortune is not living well if he is constantly filled with worry. When our mind is at ease and settled and we live a life of gratitude wherever we are, we experience the ultimate bliss, even if we are a little bit poor. But if we have a lot of money, enjoy high status, know many things, and also have a mind that is serene, then this could be called the icing on the cake. Even when we create blessings, it is even better to create them while possessing a good understanding of our mind.

We use the name "engineer" to refer to those who are good with technology, and we call people who manage others well by the name of "leader." Even these people, however, will suffer when they use their mind incorrectly. The person who controls and uses his mind well is called by the name of "practitioner of the Way" or "sage." When we use our mind well, we are able to handle technology even better and to lead people more effectively. Proper use of the mind is therefore of the utmost importance. No one who uses his mind well is incapable of managing other people. When we fail to lead others well, it is because we have not been successful in managing our own mind. For this reason, the merit of managing the mind well by seeking the *Diamond Sutra* Way is greater than anything else in this world.

The child who sees his parents' nagging as love
Will forever have devoted children.
The student capable of always hearing anew
Each and every word from the buddha's dharma seat
Will be a buddha forever carried on the back of the Buddha.

CHAPTER XXV

THE BUDDHA'S EDIFYING MIND

Edifying Without Being Edified

Heaven and earth are my front yard, the four births my family.

Whose duty is it to sweep and polish, to give medicine and pacify?

The ten-thousand-year tree is a mighty tree with no shadow.

Do you see? Its seed lies here.

"Subhuti! What do you think? You must not say that the Tathāgata thinks, 'I have properly delivered sentient beings.'"

"Subhuti! You must not entertain this thought. For the Tathāgata does not actually deliver sentient beings.

"If the Tathāgata says that he delivers sentient beings, he possesses the self notion, the person notion, the sentient being notion, and the long life notion.

"Subhuti, when the Tathāgata uses the word 'self,' it is not that a self exists. Yet ordinary humans thereby say that a self exists.

"Subhuti, in using the words 'ordinary humans,' the Tathāgata has explained that these are not ordinary humans, and he thus uses the name of 'ordinary humans.'"

Focus on

This passage teaches that although the Tathāgata delivers sentient beings, his edification bears no trace of the thought of having delivered them. There exists something that is always following us around like a shadow when we perform good works—namely, traces in the mind. This is a prideful mind. And because of this prideful mind, we suffer in the clutches of defilements and idle thoughts. Even after giving, the buddha leaves no trace of having given. I hope that the reader will learn here about the buddha mind that leaves no trace.

"Subhuti! None of you should believe that the Buddha delivers sentient beings. For in truth the tathāgata is one who bears not a trace of having delivered sentient beings. Should the tathāgata have the thought of having delivered sentient beings, that tathāgata will be bound in the four signs.

"Subhuti! When the Tathāgata referred to himself just now, it was not because he was caught in the idea of 'self.' Subhuti! The Tathāgata does not think of the ordinary human as an ordinary human. He merely calls him by the name of 'ordinary human.'"

Do Not Doubt the Buddha's Words

After achieving right enlightenment, the Buddha edified untold billions of living creatures, guiding them onto the path of progression and the path of light. The Buddha in our mind has planted in it the image of a merciful individual. Through the disciples of the Buddha, through his scriptures, and through his order, the traces of his edification have lingered in our hearts and served as the bearings for our behavior. Perhaps the Buddha is somewhere out there right now, working to deliver sentient beings. What the Buddha says here is that although he delivered a boundless number of sentient beings through this edification, he did so separately from any discriminating notion holding that "I am a buddha, and sentient beings are deluded masses in need of deliverance."

When the Buddha formed the order and guided his disciples, their numbers would likely have included some who were infatuated with the Brahman religion, some with many worldly desires, and all manner of other disciples and followers. Imagine how much effort the Buddha put into edification at this time, working directly and indirectly outside the awareness of others—sometimes admonishing his followers, sometimes praising them, sometimes remaining silent. I suspect that in edifying sentient beings in this way, he would have used expressions such as "Do as I tell you," "Do as I do," or "You must not do that." Immature disciples, however, may have heard the Buddha verbally instruct them to eliminate false notions and thought, "He seems to have the view of 'myself' and the view of 'sentient beings.'"

The Buddha teaches that he sees into this mental state among his disciples, and that although he utters words such as "This is how I am" and "My words are the truth," his words do not come from his being obscured by discriminating notions.

The whole family depends on the successful person.

When someone attains buddhahood,

the hosts of humans and heavenly beings take refuge in him.

Where do all the buddhas of past, present, and future

turn their heads?

The cries of the lonely roc echo throughout the void.

CHAPTER XXVI

THE PHYSICAL BODY AND THE DHARMAKĀYA

The Dharma Body Not Being an Appearance

Hwang-hui the minister said this was right, that was right,

and his wife was right, too.

Do not ask what is wrong.

Originally, there was only the utterly right in this land.

Child, gather up your discriminations of "seeing and not seeing properly."

"Subhuti! What do you think? Can one recognize the Tathāgata from the thirty-two marks?"

Said Subhuti, "Yes, it is so. One will recognize the Tathāgata from the thirty-two marks."

Said the Buddha, "Subhuti! Were it possible to recognize the Tathāgata from the thirty-two marks, the Cakravartin king would also be such a Tathāgata."

Said Subhuti to the Buddha, "World Honored One! From what I understand of the meaning that the Buddha has spoken, it is not possible to see the Tathāgata properly from the thirty-two marks."

At this time, the World Honored One recited a verse:

"If one sees me through form, or seeks the Tathāgata through his voice, such a person is practicing a deviant Way and will never see the Tathāgata."

Focus on

This section teaches that the buddha's character cannot be understood in terms of a physical body, and that it is achieved through knowing and training the Dharmakāya. It appears that even in the Buddha's day, a great deal of attention was paid to his outstanding physical beauty. Here, he reiterates the need to seek out and realize the Dharmakāya harbored within the mind, rather than fixating on physical appearance. Our first thought should not be of physical appearance. Rather, we must practice to pursue the nature harbored within.

"Subhuti! In your view, it is possible to recognize the buddha through seeing a physical body perfectly endowed with the thirty-two marks?"

Said Subhuti, "If he possesses the thirty-two marks, then it may indeed be said that he is a buddha."

Said the Buddha, "Subhuti! If you recognize the tathāgata from the thirty-two marks, then King Cakravartin must also be a tathāgata, for he also bore the thirty-two marks."

Said Subhuti to the Buddha, "From what I understand of the intent of the Buddha's words, it is not possible to declare that someone has the tathāgata's character simply because his external aspect is marvelous."

Worship the Dharmakāya, Not the Physical Body

Many of the houses that you see today are quite remarkable compared to the standards of the past. A remarkable house, however, does not guarantee that a remarkable owner lives there. No matter how marvelous a physical body may be, our assessment and treatment of it must differ depending on the kind of mind that uses and operates it.

It is of course true that we are only endowed with a marvelous physical body when we have accumulated many merits in previous lives and had affinities with good parents. But it is very foolish indeed to conceive of the physical body as being linked to buddhahood. The reason that the Buddha repeatedly stresses this is because disciples at the time were unable to make the distinction between an outstanding physical body and the buddha's character or truth nature.

Since time immemorial, ordinary people have judged a person's value as great or low after first viewing his physical body. After that, they have judged whether a person was good or evil from hearing his words, or from looking at his writing. Only a truly outstanding individual judges someone's character after seeing his determinations. However valuable they may be, the phenomena perceived by our sensory organs—the things seen, grasped, heard, and so forth by the six organs of our eyes, ears, nose, tongue, body, and will—are in a state of transformation. All are ultimately extinguished, and thus futile. The merciful face and appearance of the buddha are, in the end, illusory phenomena. Those who fixate on external appearance in their belief and reliance on the buddha will finally be unable to attain buddhahood—only emptiness in the face of change will remain.

In this section, then, the Buddha earnestly instructs his disciples that they must adopt as their teacher not his body, but the Dharmakāya without form or body. They must depend upon the Dharmakāya, achieve enlightenment with the Dharmakāya, and practice to recover that Dharmakāya.

At this time, the Buddha recited a verse:

"If someone seeks to encounter the buddha in this physical body,

Or seeks to find the buddha in this voice,

Such a person is practicing the dharma of action,

And will never see the tathāgata."

Find the Unpaired Object

We are entreated not to believe that someone is a buddha because he has a marvelous physical beauty, or to seek the buddha in terms of things with form, or ideas that can be pictured with the mind, as when we say, "The buddha is a buddha because of his beautiful voice."

When the person who has vowed to become a buddha thinks, "This person will be a buddha because of his outstanding physical beauty," he will focus his mind on tending to his appearance. He will work to develop a nice voice. When he views the buddha as someone with outstanding ideas, he will read many books and focus all his energies on producing ideas.

This is an earnest dharma instruction telling us that if we proceed with our cultivation in this way, substituting the buddha's characteristics into the present, tangible, changing, and non-eternal dharma of action, we are following a mistaken path that is completely different from the path toward becoming a buddha. Listen closely to the claims of religions these days, and you will find cases where they proceed with a dharma of action. These are lower-order religions, and cannot be called perfect religions. We must listen to this instruction and develop the insight to distinguish with regard to religions and figures.

There is a koan that asks, "What is that thing which is not associated with the myriad dharmas?" What this tells us is that all objects come in pairs: high and low, male and female, mountains and water. There is no object that does not have a mate, in structural terms. Yet there exists an object that is unpaired, and this is what we must seek. That unpaired object is none other than the tathāgata and Il-Won-Sang.

Show me the unpaired mind. This realm is not so difficult to reach. In terms of ease, it is a realm that can be understood with great facility. If it existed somewhere far away, we would have to travel there in search of it, but it exists closest to us in our mind. Can you see it?

Even the old, worn rubber shoe has a mate.
The sun has the moon, the heavens embrace the earth.
Lonely Zhaozhou carried a single straw shoe on his head.
The Hangang River flows into the sea, the sea into the Hangang River.

CHAPTER XXVII

THE MEANING OF 'NONEXISTENCE'
No Cessation or Extinguishing

Old Zhaozhou said at one time that the dog has a buddha nature,
And in another place that it definitely does not.
When it was in sight, he said it did not exist;
when out of sight, he said it existed.
But the prescription matches the disease,
and the prescriptions number eighty-four thousand.
It is simply that we must not be deceived by the buddha's teaching.

"Subhuti! Do you think that the Tathāgata attained Anuttara-Samyak-Sambodhi through not holding the marks of perfection?

"Subhuti! Do not think that the Tathāgata attained Anuttara-Samyak-Sambodhi through not holding the marks of perfection.

"Subhuti! Would you said, 'For he who has produced the Anuttara-Samyak-Sambodhi mind, all dharmas have been extinguished and ceased'?

"Do not entertain this thought. For he who has produced the Anuttara-Samyak-Sambodhi mind does not speak of the notion of ceasing and extinguishing all dharmas."

Focus on

The tathāgata realized the unsurpassed great Way by training with a method of mind use that is unobstructed by being or nonbeing. Once we begin practice toward becoming a buddha, we have the impression that we are being taught of the need to "abandon this" and "eliminate that." We must have a very clear understanding of the meaning of this negation. I hope that you will learn through this chapter about the ultimate Way that cannot be said to exist and cannot be said not to exist.

"Subhuti! Do you think that the Tathāgata has attained the unsurpassed great Way through having denied that he is perfectly endowed? Subhuti! Do not entertain this thought.

"Subhuti! Would you say that the person who has resolved to attain the unsurpassed great Way and cultivates the Way must sever and eliminate all sensory conditions and all valuable things? Do not entertain this thought.

"For the person who practices after resolving to attain the unsurpassed great Way does not believe that cutting off and eliminating in response to all sensory conditions is everything, nor is he caught by the idea of no trace existing."

The Tathāgata Realm Is Not a Realm of Nonexistence

Because it is said that the tathāgata is a realm of nonbeing, the person who has not awakened to the Way may believe that one is following the Way when one has no mind, and may fall away into the realm of nonexistence. By mistake, we may lapse into the realm of nonexistence and fall into dead emptiness. This dharma instruction delivers a warning to the person who has seen the nature incorrectly.

Ordinary sentient beings fixate on the existing. They are drawn to those things where substance is visible and minds are present. Those engaged in Theravāda practice mainly practice elimination, while those who engage in Supreme Vehicle practice are said to adopt the standard of free command of existence and nonexistence. But the person who has not seen the nature with certainty will often conclude that the realm is the one where minds have ceased—where there is nothing. When he experiences an incorrect awakening to that realm of true suchness and errs with his practice, he will often end up merely compounding his ignorance. Seeing the nature does not consist of this kind of elimination. This is a somewhat difficult section of the Sutra.

Long ago, the Sixth Patriarch Huineng was visited by a disciple who reported having witnessed someone who had seen the nature. Huineng asked, "How did this person sing about having experienced the nature?" The disciple recited the verse for him:

"Wolun possesses a talent;

He has succeeded in disconnecting all thought.

He experiences no mind even toward sensory conditions.

With each day, the mind of enlightenment grows."

Hearing this, Huineng stated flatly that this person had not seen the nature. Then he recited his own verse:

"Huineng possesses no talent;

The one hundred thoughts he cannot halt.

His mind arises in response to conditions.

How could the mind of enlightenment grow?

Despite the words "nonbeing" and "nothingness," this is not a realm of nonexistence. It is a realm that contains all things completely.

There is an interesting anecdote from long ago about seeking the Way. An old woman was intently devoted to her practice. She honored a monk, giving him offerings and encouraging him to practice intently. Twenty years passed, and she decided to test the monk. She dressed up her pretty daughter and sent her into his room with the instruction to embrace him from behind. And she told the daughter to ask him a question. The daughter did as she was told. She went into the room, embraced the monk, and asked, "Venerable One, what is your mind right now?"

The monk replied, "Right now, my mind is like a withered tree and utterly free of thought."

The maiden went to her mother and reported what the monk had said. Enraged, the old woman shouted, "For twenty years I made offerings to that swine! I spent two decades giving offerings to that idiot monk!"

She proceeded to drive the monk away and burn the temple to the ground. His answer shows that he had certainly fallen into the realm of nonbeing. Still, would it show that he had seen the nature if he had said, "Your body is warm and soft"? It is said that such questions were posed as a way of testing whether one had seen the nature incorrectly. It is a mistake, however, to believe that seeing the nature means having no mind, having an extinguished mind. The realm in question is perfect and complete—filled with grace, filled with wisdom, and filled with creative transformations. But when we are compelled to express that realm in words, we speak of "nonbeing." This is the truth of namelessness, not a realm of nonexistence through extinguishing. As such, it is a mistake for any of the practitioners of the past, present, and future to misunderstand this realm.

We call our child "my puppy" because he is precious.
We call him "darling" in our joy at seeing him.
When you are not sure of the truth, look to your inner buddha.
The wise person looks at neither the finger nor the void-moon.

CHAPTER XXVIII

TO FREEDOM
Neither Receiving Nor Coveting

How brilliant, the great object of nature.
The sun and moon pale in comparison,
Tusita Heaven is no more than my home.
Its breath is a typhoon, it speaks through the four seasons.
To narrowly escape pollution is one of its lesser talents.

"Subhuti! Even if the bodhisattva were to use enough of the seven treasures to fill as many worlds as there are grains of sand in the Ganges River for charitable service, if another person attains the realization of perseverance through awareness of absence of self in all dharmas, this bodhisattva would enjoy more merits that those gained by the aforementioned bodhisattva.

"For Subhuti! All bodhisattvas do not receive blessings and merits."

Said Subhuti to the Buddha, "World Honored One! Why do you say the bodhisattva does not receive blessings and merits?"

"Subhuti! The bodhisattva rightly does not cling greedily to the blessings and merits that he has created, and for this reason I teach that he does not receive blessings and merits."

Focus on

In this section, the Buddha shows that the bodhisattva who has realized the dharma of selflessness achieves liberation from blessings and merits, and thereby commands them at will. Imagine how much effort goes into awakening to the realm of selflessness and training oneself until that realm is one's own. This chapter teaches that the person who has made the dharma of selflessness his own is never tainted by, or fixated on, exchange. I hope that you will study this well.

"Subhuti! If one bodhisattva were to perform charitable services with enough of the seven treasures to fill as many worlds as there are grains of sand in the Ganges River, and others were to awaken to and realize the dharma of selflessness, it may be said that the merits of these latter bodhisattvas are far greater even than those of the first bodhisattva. For Subhuti! All these bodhisattvas have achieved liberation from blessings and are thus capable of using them at will."

Making the Realm of Buddha Nature Our Own

In this section, the Buddha explains the state of the mind without obstruction or hindrance by any sensory conditions, which is gained through disciplining the tathāgata realm.

At this point, he has explained that the merits of gaining that realm—the dharma of selflessness—and of practicing it and sharing it with others are far greater than even those from charitable giving with the seven treasures.

It is worth considering why the word "perseverance" is used in describing awakening to and realizing the realm of selflessness. I believe that the Buddha used the word "perseverance" because he is describing how realization of the realm came from persevering through sensory conditions and recovering that realm, persevering further and recovering that realm, recovering that realm even when happy, and persevering and recovering even under difficult circumstances.

When someone sees the nature of the pure Dharmakāya Buddha realm and has precisely emulated that realm, he is said to have realized the perfect Sambhogakāya. Just as we stamp a document to testify to its accuracy, we are said to have achieved realization and gotten our stamp when we declare that the realm to which we have awakened is exactly the same as the one to which the buddha awakened, and that we have made it our own. This attainment of a stamp is very important.

When a person achieves the status of "Dharma Strong and Māra Defeated," he may guarantee that he will not commit wicked deeds in this lifetime, and that he will not succumb to temptation or commit transgressions even when confronted by adverse conditions. But he can make no guarantees for the next life. It is possible that his inability to practice over a long period of time—while in his mother's womb, and as a child—could lead to his erring and going astray.

When we practice at the status of "Beyond the Household," we realize the power that is gathered amply within that realm. So firm and strong is this power that we may achieve liberation through repeated practice in the next life as well without being darkened. For this reason, we will need to achieve the status of Beyond the

Household in this life rather than that of Māra Defeated.

It is said that a rocket fired into the sky is subject to the pull of gravity while it remains within the atmosphere, but that it is no longer constrained once it escapes. When we have achieved the status of Māra Defeated, we are laboring to stay in orbit within the atmosphere. When we ascend to the status of Beyond the Household, however, we proceed outside the atmosphere and can freely tour the world without difficulty. All of this is owing to the powers that we have realized.

There was a monk who always used to say, "I'm so busy! I'm so busy!" It is said that as the monks were performing funeral rites after his death, they said, "Venerable Busy One will surely be at peace and no longer be so busy now that he has passed away." At this, a voice rang out in the void, crying, "I'm still busy!" As we live our lives, we are busy making a living, busy washing clothes and combing our hair, busy comforting people when something happens to them. But what should we busy ourselves with more? Tending to our mind. Thus, the person who cultivates the Way minimizes his efforts at tending to his possessions. He must reduce the number of things that he is compelled to look after and busy himself with looking after his mind.

At the very least, we should work feverishly to tend to our mind-practice after we have reached the age of forty. We must tend to it today and tend to it tomorrow, so that the numinous elixir clusters together. Only when the numinous elixir clusters together can we escape from the ideas and notions that have arisen from the sensory conditions of the five desires and the minions of Māra.

The Power to Command Natural and Fixed Karma

Two types of karma exist: natural karma and fixed karma. With natural karma, the truth binds ordinary humans and sentient beings so that they cannot move. Men are designed to like women. It is even said that when a man dies, he follows female mourners in his rebirth. In this way, women are designed to like men, and men to like women. The truth has made it so. *yang* proceeds toward *yin*, and *yin* proceeds toward *yang*. Thus, ordinary humans and sentient beings are made to be manipulated by this. Very rare indeed is the person who has broken free from it.

Fighting is futile. President, inventor, famous painter—all are carried along by natural karma. We are all the same in being unable to break through this, albeit with some degree of difference.

Fixed karma, in contrast, was created in previous lives. Think of a man who died, leaving someone whom he cared for behind. When they were reborn in this life, however, there was a difference in ages because they died at different times. He grew older and met another woman through natural karma, and the two of them married. Suddenly, this other woman appeared with whom he was connected through fixed karma. What happens in this situation? By mistake, he could be drawn by the power of fixed karma, abandoning the wife whom he married through natural karma and acting in accordance with his fixed karma from his previous life. This fixed karma is a very fearsome thing. Our vision is obscured, and we cannot see properly.

A crown prince once gave up the throne for the sake of a woman whom he loved. Generally, those who have been unable to defeat Māra become the playthings of natural karma and fixed karma. We ride up and down on the seesaw of these two forms of karma. But when we awaken to and realize the realm that is ever calm and ever alert, we gain the ability to go through our life with a command over fixed and natural karma.

When we do so, we are said to have achieved freedom and liberation. For this reason, those who go through life controlling *yin* and *yang* and commanding natural and fixed karma are described as sages. We must begin our efforts toward achieving this. For only in that way will we be able to command fixed karma without being bound by it, even after we are married. What must we do to be able to go through life with such a command? We will only be capable of doing so when we have awakened to the ever-calm and ever-alert realm, and work constantly to recover it and keep it with us.

There is one *Won*-Buddhist hymn that I particularly like. Its words are as follows:

"The rain fell on a lotus leaf, and only a bead rolled down.

Where are the traces of all the rain that fell?

If this mind is the same way, it becomes the Lotus Pedestal."

A lotus leaf has a slick surface. As a result, the drops of rain that fall on it do not soak through, but roll away. What if we had minds that were also like lotus leaves? How happy we would be to have a mind that is forever free, even when the rain falls on the lotus leaf: when a sad mind comes, we make the appropriate choice and it rolls away, and when pleasant sensory conditions come, they vanish as well. When such a person is in hell, it is not hell. When he is in prison, it is not a prison.

After Dosan Yi Dong-an, one of our forerunners, passed away, the Founding Master is said to have uttered these words in his grief:

"I should be this sad when Dosan has died."

The Founding Master's words indicate that he has the strength of mind to be this way when he wishes to be this way, and to be that way when he wishes to be that way. Confucius, too, said something similar when Yan Hui died. Even someone like Confucius can achieve this through discipline. As for us, we are unable to operate our minds as we wish. Once our mind has been unsettled, we may feel good or feel bad for days at a time.

There was one truly remarkable individual (someone who achieved awakening), though not so famous. I went to visit him just before he passed away, and he calmly said to me, "What is life or death to the practitioner? What is pain?" It seemed as though he had recovered that realm. We must do the same. A person may only be called a true practitioner of the Way when he preserves that just-as-it-is mind even when dying beneath a stained quilt.

Is it Chuangtze's pain in the butterfly's dream,
Or the butterfly's dance in Chuangtze's dream?
They all say to wake from the dream,
But even the buddha wanders in the dream
of delivering sentient beings.
The six destinies and four births are all travelers in a dream.
Practitioner, pray you dream beautiful dreams.
When you know the dream for a dream,
you know there will be no taint.

INTERPRETATION

Said Subhuti to the Buddha, "World Honored One! What do you mean in saying that they do not receive blessings and merits?"

"Subhuti! The blessings and merits created by the bodhisattva do not stem from greed or attachment. For this reason, I am saying that he is not tainted by blessings and merits."

Not Tainted by Temptation

In concrete terms, the words "not receiving blessings and merits" mean that we do not fixate on the mind even in a pleasing environment, nor do we bow to the mind even amid a torturous environment. Many blessings come to the person who has created many blessings. Ordinary humans become intoxicated with the blessings that come, and grow arrogant. As this builds up, it turns into transgression. But when the practitioner receives blessings, he is not tainted even as he receives them.

One of the most distressing things for us is the suffering that arises from encountering those we resent and hate. For example, we may live with a hated person. Parting with someone whom we are fond of can be a treasured memory and something beautiful, but when we live like the person who hates, our bowels are in a knot and hateful minds spew forth from our entire being.

When we have no hateful minds even when we live with a hateful person, this is what is meant by "not receiving blessings." It could also be restated as "not receiving hatred and love." And when we live with people whom we love, loving minds emerge from our entire being, making us feel warm just being next to such people. This is not an entirely good thing. When we do so, we are unable to part from such a person after we die, and we end up wandering about. For this reason, we must have the dharma power not to let our minds be swayed even when we are next to someone whom we love.

A loving mind is not at all a bad thing. We simply must not let ourselves be swayed by that mind, or commit transgressions or lose our freedom owing to its influence. I sometimes paint orchids. I go to sleep after painting a flower, and the next morning there immediately arises in me a mind to paint orchids. A mind emerges that wishes to paint a picture before performing seated meditation. The same thing happens when we die. If we die while our mind is fixated on someone, our soul proceeds toward that person—just as I wish to paint an orchid the next day when I fall asleep before finishing. When we fall asleep after spending an evening trying and failing to solve some problem, a mind to do so arises suddenly in the morning. We become like this when we die. Once you have done something, you should erase it before you go to sleep. You may try seated meditation, but in any case you should make sure to erase it. Not receiving blessings means adjusting without love or hate in response to sensory conditions of love and hate.

I practice calligraphy, so I will use that as an example. When you practice calligraphy for any length of time, you will encounter profane writing. It gives an unpleasant sensation when you look at it, and cannot be hung on the wall. Now, Master Taesan was an outstanding calligrapher. One day, he saw a profanely written piece of calligraphy and said, "That's very good." It seems that he had a great liking for it because it was brought by a follower with great sincerity. In this way, there is no "good" or "bad." We can always let go of it as needed.

Not receiving blessings means experiencing freedom amid adverse and favorable conditions, freedom amid hatred and love, freedom amid suffering and pleasure, and freedom amid life and death. One of Master Taesan's writings says the following:

"On Mt. Jaunsan

There is a monk who is deaf and dumb.

He experiences the mind arising when conditions come

And the mind extinguishing when conditions go."

All of you should become like this monk. When someone has gathered that realm well in his mind, he is said to be like someone who is deaf and mute. Those who gather the realm in this way become the deaf and mute monk. You must develop the dharma power so that when conditions are present, you produce the right thoughts to resolve them, and when they disappear, they are able to vanish without a trace.

CHAPTER XXIX

THAT MIND GOING, THAT MIND COMING

His Demeanor Being Serene and Tranquil

When we go, it is that land; when we come, it is that mind.

Even amid the coming and going, then, too, it is just that object.

It is a calculation that cannot be fathomed

in terms of adding, subtracting, multiplying, and dividing.

When you are thirsty, drink water; when you are sleepy, get some rest.

"Subhuti! Should someone say, 'The Tathāgata comes and goes, sits and lies down,' this person has not understood the intent of my teachings.

"For the tathāgata neither comes from anywhere nor goes anywhere, and thus is called by the name of 'Tathāgata.'"

Focus on

The mind that is without change even when sensory conditions come from outside, the true mind that is without change even when sensory conditions depart—this constant mind is the mind of the buddha. The Buddha taught that such a mind is called "tathāgata." We experience torment or pleasure because of the ever-changing minds that arise in response to the conditions that we encounter. With this chapter, I hope that you will focus your sincere commitment on finding the mind without change and taming it so that it is your chief mind at all times.

"Subhuti! If someone says that the Tathāgata comes and goes, sits and lies down, such a person does not understand well the true meaning of which the Tathāgata speaks. For the Tathāgata is said to be a tathāgata when he is ever with the myriad dharmas without coming or going."

The One Thing That Does Not Change Even As All Things Change

Do you know of the body's changes? You may not sense the body gradually aging and sickening when you are young, but once you have reached a certain age you become acutely aware of the aging process.

The body changes, and affinities also change. People who were once close to us grow more and more distant when they are far away. You may not have known someone well before, but developed an attachment after encountering him frequently. Encounters with people are rarely pure and simple encounters.

I had a dog when I was in Yeongsan. That dog was only happy when it was given something. Objects became a medium for its pleasure and displeasure.

Reader! What do you do when you encounter someone?

"I like you because I'm lonely."

"I like you because you have money."

When people encounter others, they inevitably put something in between them. And the relationship changes as the thing in between them changes.

Things change according to our values, and they change according to our circumstances. Affinities are truly impermanent.

The mind, too, is impermanent. Even a firm vow is impermanent. And the mind changes more than anything. True, the physical body changes over the years, but the mind changes from moment to moment. Even a firm vow only resists change when we continuously say, "It must not change, it must not change." Otherwise, it will change again when we proceed to the next life.

Our lives are like a ride on a moving train. While all things are changing, there exists one unchanging realm, and that is the tathāgata realm. The tathāgata realm is just so when conditions come, and just so when conditions go. It is just as it is when happiness comes, it is just as it is when misfortune comes, it is just as it is when happiness goes, and it is just as it is when misfortune goes. For this reason, we say "thus come, thus gone."

> Tathāgata who neither sits nor lies down,
>
> who neither comes nor goes.
>
> Who shall come to give buddha offerings
>
> to the wooden Buddha?
>
> Buddhist, listen closely and understand.
>
> The Tathāgata comes and goes, laughs and cries, and all that.

Practice to Preserve the Tathāgata Realm

The process of buddhas awakening to the Way and disciplining themselves with that realm is described as "practice with keeping one's mind from internal disturbances and external temptations." This term refers to the preservation and protection of that realm. The Buddha called this "thus come, thus gone," while Laotze said, "The valley spirit must never die—we carry on disciplining that place—scrupulous and continuous like a cotton thread, as though just present."

The Founding Master expressed this by saying "one suchness in action and rest," meaning that we must continue with the same one mind at all times, whether active or resting. There is another expression: "Never losing that realm even when we have let go of a mind, and never fixating even when we have seized that realm."

We must discover our mind-ground. And we must never let go of that mind.

Regrettably, sentient beings do lose that mind. This happens for three reasons. The first is unawareness. Even when we are aware, we become tainted, and the mind-ground is hidden. This is the second stumbling block, and the third way we lose that mind is through fixation. These three stumbling blocks necessarily arise when we are coming and going in life and death, and when we are living our lives. We must exert ourselves in efforts to overcome them.

Laotze expressed this mind-ground very nicely with the term "valley spirit." A valley is empty, yet it is also oddly numinous. Thus he described it as the "valley spirit." We must not kill this valley spirit realm. We kill it through unawareness, through being tainted, and through fixation, and we are told not to do so, but to be scrupulous and continous like a cotton thread, as though just present. When we discipline it in this way, it becomes the jewel of eternal life, and when numinous elixir clusters come together it forms the life of all buddhas of past, present, and future. Those who do not understand this cannot be the buddhas of past, present, and future. And only when this is present can we be free to do as we will, and thus create blessings.

There are times when clerics wish to deliver a dharma instruction, yet are unable to clearly articulate what they want to say. At such times, they gather their minds and recover that realm through seated meditation or formal prayer, and the instruction begins to emerge. It is just like clearing away the mud that fills a spring.

Some people, when told to give a dharma instruction, will go searching through their books. This is like hunting crabs with someone else's lantern. The person who possesses his own lantern makes the wisdom of the books that he reads into something of his own. The person who does not will be darkened before long when he reads books, just as when you hunt crabs with someone else's lantern. Like a magic wand that produces anything you want, the tathāgata realm, once gathered well, can be used for this and that purpose. This is referred to as "practice toward not leaving the self-nature."

One of the Buddha's ten main disciples was a monk by the name of Śāriputra. This monk possessed formidable wisdom. While *The Diamond Sutra* is a dialogue with Subhuti, *The Heart Sutra* is a dialogue with Śāriputra. This monk was on his way to the city when he saw a follower coming out, a woman named Candrottara who had practiced a great deal.

"Where are you going?" asked Śāriputra.

"I am going where you are going," answered Candrottara.

"But aren't you leaving, and aren't I going in?" asked Śāriputra.

And Candrottara, perhaps because she had practiced so much, asked, "Where do the monks of great dharma in the past, present, and future always abide as they live?"

"They abide in unbounded liberation nirvana," answered Śāriputra.

Said Candrottara, "Then am I not following the same road?"

Where do you abide as you live your life? It is very important that you find the tathāgata realm of nirvana and abide in that realm as you live. When you abide in anything else—in desire, in wicked minds, in your own success, in your own kindness, in your own purity—the seeds of torment are germinated. We must abide in the void mind where no abiding is possible and go through our lives commanding the buddhadharma, commanding riches, and commanding virtuous capabilities.

The realm that is always replenished however much one eats,
The billion defilements and billion wisdoms,
Dragon-Heaven spring water that never runs dry.
Do not stand around begging from the buddha.
Everything is right there. Tsk tsk tsk.

CHAPTER XXX

THE TRUTH IS ONE
The Principle Image of One Unity

The drawing on white paper is the itinerary for delivering sentient beings.

When you have understood, you will erase it in an instant.

Drawing the picture and erasing it again, all limitless mercy.

Why don't those of us without cares gather and perhaps climb a spring hill?

"Subhuti! What do you think would happen if the virtuous man or woman were to smash the Three Thousand Great Thousand Worlds into specks of dust? Would you say that the specks of dust would be great in number?"

Said Subhuti, "Very great, World Honored One! For if these specks truly exist, the Buddha would not say that they are these specks.

"This is because the specks spoken of by the Buddha are not specks, and thus they are called by the name of 'specks of dust.'

"World Honored One! Even the Three Thousand Great Thousand Worlds of which the Tathāgata spoke is not a world, and thus is called by the name of 'world.'

"For if the world exists, it is the one unity image. But even the one unity image of which the Tathāgata spoke is not the one unity image, and thus is called by the name of 'one unity image.'"

"Subhuti! The one unity image cannot be taught, yet ordinary humans cling to it greedily."

Focus on

Within the specks of the "small realm" that make up the world and the great realm of the whole, there exists a truth that unifies them into a single whole. We are told that this is the "one unity image," but that is the kind of realm that lacks any defined form. In this chapter, I hope you will learn with certainty the meaning of the "one unity image" and study about the way in which the practitioner seeks it.

"Subhuti! Do you think that if the virtuous man or woman smashed the whole of this universe into specks of dust, the specks would be numerous?"

"I would say that they would be extremely numerous, World Honored One! Even if the clouds of dust of which you just spoke were something truly existing, you could not say that they are simply specks of dust, for they do not exist outside the truth. You merely refer to them by the name of 'specks of dust.'"

All Defilements Are the Way

The "specks of dust" in *The Diamond Sutra* refer to all objects. The number of different objects in this world is truly vast. All those objects are vast in number when viewed individually. But each speck of dust harbors within it a buddha nature of true suchness. By themselves, objects are many, but because they are all manifestations of the truth in terms of their origin, they could be described as specks of the truth. In other words, it would be proper to describe them as "truthful specks," and we merely call them "all objects" and "specks" because that is what the people of the world do. The individual objects are all different, but the truth that flows within them is one. What you must instill deeply from this chapter is that although all objects are just objects, a single truth is harbored within them.

Examine your own mind kingdom. Within your mind, innumerable sentient-being minds—defilements and idle thoughts— are coming and going. They rise and subside like waves on the ocean. From where do these defilements and idle thoughts arise? They arise from the original nature of true suchness. And their emergence and extinguishing are all manifestations of principle. They are principle manifesting itself. So although they are defilements, they are not defilements; they are merely minds that are not suited to this particular time and place.

All the objects in this world bear different names. But the Dharmakāya Buddha is harbored within those things, and all the transformations of these objects take place through the workings of the Dharmakāya Buddha. Thus objects and defilements, as numerous as specks of dust, are all based in the Dharmakāya realm. They are therefore things that cannot be neglected, and they are by necessity dharma flowers. We merely call these objects "specks of dust" because that is what the world does.

"World Honored One! The 'whole of the universe' of which the Tathāgata just spoke is in reality formed from specks gathered together. Thus we cannot insist on its being the whole of the universe. We merely call it the 'world' as a term in common usage.

"But if the whole of the universe be grounded in a true principle, it may be said that its image is that of the truth world and the real world combined into one. Yet even this one unity image is not fixed through any definition. It is called by the name of 'one unity image' to express the inexpressible."

"Subhuti! The 'one unity image' principle cannot be defined as anything in words, yet ordinary humans seek that realm in their craving."

See the Picture That Cannot Be Painted

The Founding Master said that when the small individual entities of the realm of the phenomenal (the small realm) come together, they form the great realm, or the realm of the absolute—that is, the realm of the whole. The Buddha uses the word "world" to refer to this whole. To describe it from a different angle, the great realm refers to the truth realm, while the small realm describes phenomena. He says that when we explain both the great realm and the small realm together, this is the one unity image.

In *The Heart Sutra*, we find the words "Form does not differ from the void." Form, here, refers to the phenomenal, the small realm, while the void refers to the true suchness—that is, the great realm of the buddha. The truth realm is no different from the realm of the phenomenal.

We also find the words, "Form is void, and void is form." In other words, the truth realm and the realm of the phenomenal are no different, but one and the same. In a word, this tells us that there is no phenomenon outside the truth and no truth outside phenomena. In *The Diamond Sutra*, the term "one unity image" refers to these together.

There once was a person who asked, "What is the great principle of the buddha's dharma?"

"It is the nut pine in front of the yard," came the explanation.

Another person said, "It is the dung-cleaning stick."

In an elaboration, Master Taesan said that this expression did a very good job of explaining the realm of buddha nature.

The truth is not something that exists separately from reality. It is not a god in heaven, but a god harbored within the whole of the universe. We produce defilements and idle thoughts, we produce all manner of unnecessary minds, but in truth those defilements are supreme enlightenment, and so the mind is no different from defilements.

There are two kinds of buddha offerings that we perform. When we perform buddha offerings for the whole, these are called "truth buddha offerings." And when we make buddha offerings to the small realm, they are called "specific object buddha offerings." When we speak of both of these together, specific object buddha offerings and truth buddha offerings, we simply call them "buddha offerings." The Buddha used the term "one unity image," combining phenomena and the truth into a single whole. The Founding Master Sot'aesan portrayed the one unity image with an image—that of the Il-Won-Sang. It suffices to understand that he was developing the buddhadharma in a modern style.

I sometimes made portraits of Bodhidharma while I was living in Cheongju. By dint of its location near Mt. Songnisan, Cheongju was a place where Buddhism flourished. A monk had asked for a portrait, and I showed a circular image behind Bodhidharma. I depicted the circle in the image of Bodhidharma radiating the light. The monk said the circular image was nice, and so I composed a verse for it.

"The Il-Won-Sang Buddha has no form.

There is nothing in heaven and earth that he cannot do.

Where shall we hear the news of the Il-Won-Sang?

Outside the window, there is only the scattered falling of snow."

The Il-Won-Sang is merely an image. The important thing is to see the realm through it.

CHAPTER XXXI

THE VIEWS OF THE BUDDHA

Not Producing Knowledge and Views

When Confucius comes, the dogs howl wildly.

When the roc flies, the crow hides its food.

Let it go; what does it matter if you do this or that?

Moonlight alone fills the vast seas and long rivers.

"Subhuti! Suppose a person were to say, 'The Buddha has spoken the 'self' view, the 'person' view, the 'sentient being' view, and 'long life' view.

"Subhuti! What do you think? Would you say this person has understood the meaning of my words?"

"No. World Honored One! This person does not understand the meaning that the Tathāgata has spoken. For the self view, person view, sentient being view, and long life view uttered by the World Honored One are not in fact the self view, person view, sentient being view, or long life view, and so they are called by the names of 'self view,' 'other view,' 'sentient being view,' and 'long life view.'

"Subhuti! If the one who has produced the Anuttara-Samyak-Sambodhi mind properly understands in this way, sees in this way, and believes and knows in this way with regard to all dharmas, he should not produce dharma notions.

"Subhuti! When the Tathāgata speaks the words 'dharma notions,' these are not dharma notions, and so he calls them by the name of 'dharma notions.'"

Focus on

In this section, the Buddha shows that because the tathāgata presents his knowledge and perspective without being bound to language, names, and signs, we must practice with this as our standard. The language of sentient beings consists of expressions out of fixation, whereas the buddha's language is produced for the purpose of teaching. It appears that sentient beings suspected the Buddha of fixating on views because they merely listened to his words and failed to understand them. I hope that the reader will master and understand the language without fixation that is used according to pure need.

"Subhuti! If a person says that the Buddha has spoken in certain cases of the concept of 'myself,' the concept of 'you,' or the concept of 'sentient being' or 'long life,' can it be said that this person has understood the intentions of the Buddha's words?"

"No. Such a person does not clearly understand the Buddha's method of mind use. For the concept of 'myself,' the concept of 'you,' and the concept of 'sentient being' or 'long life' spoken by the Buddha are not uttered out of fixation on concepts or notions. They are used as names for the purpose of teaching the dharma."

The Buddha's Boasting Is Not Boasting, But Instruction

In giving his dharma discourse, the Buddha frequently speaks of "you" and "I," and on occasion he expresses great love or concern for his children. Seeing this, ordinary humans and sentient beings would ask, "Is this buddha not bound to self views, person views, and long life views?" This is a response to such questions.

The Buddha had a son named Rahula, a name that translates as "stumbling block." Even after being ordained, Rahula frequently defied the precepts and engaged in mischief. The Buddha became concerned and summoned his son. He asked his son to wash his feet. After Rahula finished, there was some water left in the basin, and the Buddha told his son to drink the water. Rahula said that the water was dirty, and that he would not drink it. When asked why he refused to drink, he said that he could not drink dirty water, even if it had been used to wash the feet of the Buddha. The Buddha then told him to pour the water out and bring the basin. He proceeded to instruct his son to put rice in the basin and eat it. Rahula said that he could not put rice in a dirty basin. And the Buddha said:

"Have you not often violated the precepts?"

"I have."

"When you violated the precepts, it is as though a washing basin was befouled. That is why there is no one around you. Do you wish to be defiled in this way? You will only be a clean person when you uphold the precepts well."

Seeing this expression of love for his son, students of the Buddha may believe that he, too, fixated on his child. Trivial matters such as this may be present in the environment of the Buddha. For this reason, we must understand that there is a difference between the way in which the buddha loves and the way in which sentient beings love.

In *The Diamond Sutra*, we find much boasting from the Buddha. He declares repeatedly that his words are infallible and contain no falsehood. In a sense, he is praising himself. But his words here differ from the boasting of sentient beings, as they are intended to instruct his disciples.

I was talking with someone whose son was a source of great concern. We were sharing concerns, and the discussion subtly shifted over to boasting about the son: "Even so, our son has done this and that." Another person who was expressing concern about her husband followed suit, and the topic changed to boasting of her husband. One might say that the concerns that sentient beings express for their children turn into fixation and prevent them from holding right views. But when buddhas worry for and love their children, they do so while holding right views.

During his time as a government official, Confucius had a man named Shao Zhengmao put to death. But it is worth considering whether Confucius did so out of hatred for the man. When sentient beings kill out of hatred, it is different from Confucius killing by necessity for the sake of the country. Confucius discriminated on occasion, and the Buddha also discriminated. But even when discriminating, they did so in the right way for that particular setting, based on an empty mind.

As I read this section, I feel that the Buddha must have been truly happy with a disciple like Subhuti.

I envy Subhuti, someone who lived as one with the Buddha— one mind, one thought, one breath, and one feeling. It is difficult to become a teacher, but I believe it is also quite difficult to be a smart student. We should connect in a single mind and become disciples like Subhuti who truly know the Buddha. Only by truly knowing the teacher, I think, can we carry the dharma forward. We consider whether ours is a relationship between teacher and student that transcends understanding. As we form affinities within the buddhadharma, we inevitably drift further away when we view it in terms of interests. At the very least, we should become students of the buddha who rise above matters of personal interest. Just as we rise above interests in a family relationship, so, too, should we rise above interests when forming affinities within Buddhism.

> The sentient being loves, and the buddha loves.
> What is different between the two?
> A single speck in the eye and a flower
> blooms ostentatiously in the void.
> It is so. The elimination of even that one speck is
> the buddhadharma.

"Subhuti! The person who has set the aspiration of attaining buddhahood will learn the notionless method of using the mind taught by the Tathāgata in response to all sensory conditions. He will observe that realm, and he must believe in it and awaken to it, realizing it through cultivation of the great Way of no-action, but without being bound to that dharma notion.

"Subhuti! When I speak the words 'dharma notion,' it is not because the foundation of the dharma notion exists. It is merely the name of 'dharma notion.'"

The Buddha's Method of Mind Use

The goal of all buddhas who came to this world, the work that all sages arrive on this Earth to do, and the work of all religions on this planet are ultimately to guide people to live better lives. When all of you dedicate part of your precious time to studying *The Diamond Sutra*, this, too, is in the hope of living a better life. What we pursue when we seek to live well is, ultimately, the ability to feel peace of mind in all times and places, and the ability to be pleased and peaceful no matter whom we encounter. This is not something that can be achieved externally through scholarship, honors, power, or economic means. It is only possible when we discipline our own mind well.

Ultimately, then, mind-practice is the only way to live well. In this passage, the Buddha tells us that if we set the aspiration of achieving unsurpassed and perfect enlightenment, we must start by doing as we have been taught thus far when encountering any sensory conditions. That is to say, first establishing an empty mind without dwelling, and then producing the right thoughts for the situation and acting accordingly ("giving rise to the mind that, even while responding, does not abide anywhere"), or else recovering the endlessly calm mind and producing discriminating minds suited to that time and place. ("allowing discriminations to be from the dharma of no-action"). We must achieve this awakening, and we must make judgments about the affairs of the world according to the teachings of the Buddha, believing in and awakening to the mind that is free of notions, and putting that mind into practice. The Buddha also entreats us not to generate the prideful idea that we are putting the buddhadharma into practice well, simply because we have achieved some small degree of practice in this way.

We must not simply hear *The Diamond Sutra* once and forget about it, like the proverbial dog passing by the rock. We only become a true student of the Buddha when we awaken to what the core use of the mind in *The Diamond Sutra* is and tend to it—constantly reciting, writing, and praying as we vow to put it into practice—and when we possess the bold resolution and determination to act at all times according to the *Diamond Sutra* method of mind use when we encounter conditions.

We should be practicing students of the Buddha who put the buddhadharma into practice ourselves, not the faith-practice students who are content only to believe. And we should be higher-level students of deliverance practice who teach the buddhadharma to others rather than merely practicing it by ourselves.

The brilliant dharma instructions,
like the silk of the buddha and enlightened masters,
The stars are all oriented toward the Pole Star.
Where should the Pole Star itself be oriented?
The lone goose from the south flies off to the west. *Katsu!*

CHAPTER XXXII

A PLEA FOR EDIFICATION

The Transformation Body Not Being the True Body

The master orders me to venture forth and do as he does.

Is it not a sacred endeavor over an eternity of lives?

With believing lives like all the grains of sand in the Ganges,

A merry dance, perhaps, to the flute with no holes.

"Subhuti! Even if someone used enough of the seven treasures to fill innumerable asaṃkhyeyas of worlds for charitable service, if a virtuous man or woman who has produced the mind of supreme enlightenment receives and upholds, reads and recites this sutra and speaks even only its four-line gathas to others, the blessings would surpass those of the former. How are we to speak it to others? We must not grasp notions, and we must be unmoving in suchness. For all of the conditioned dharmas are like dreams and illusions, like bubbles and shadows, like dew and lightning. He will regard them in this way."

When Buddha finished teaching the sutra, the Venerable Subhuti and all the bhikṣus and bhikṣunīs, upāsakas and upāsikās, and all the heavenly beings and asuras in all the worlds, in their great joy at having have heard the Buddha's teachings, believed in it and accepted it, revered it, and put it into practice.

Focus on

This is the final section of *The Diamond Sutra.* In this dharma instruction, the Buddha tells us that neither the life of material values nor the life of charitable service through material things alone can give eternal happiness, and that it is ultimately only through the performance of mind-practice without form that we can truly practice to live well. He also earnestly entreats us to teach mind-practice without fixation to others. I hope that you will consider whether you have experienced and realized the Dharmakāya, reflect on how much sincere effort you are putting into spreading the buddhadharma, and vow to edify others through this dharma.

"Subhuti, even if someone performs charitable service with enough of the seven treasures to fill countless worlds, someone who has resolved to achieve the unsurpassed great Way and reads, recites, practices, and delivers speeches to others on just the four-line gathas of *The Diamond Sutra* will enjoy far greater blessings than those."

Principal Values and Incidental Values

We cannot obtain eternal happiness within material existence. The Buddha once again conclusively emphasizes that we can never be eternally happy with a life spent adopting material values as our principal values.

I often read about people in the newspaper or see people on television who take pride in the performance of charitable acts for others and emphasize this as a societal value. Perhaps the people engaged in charity efforts for others would be bewildered to hear this dharma instruction from *The Diamond Sutra*.

Ordinary people aspire first and foremost to material wealth. They expend efforts to attain things, sometimes using the strangest means. And once they come to possess such things, they invest a tremendous amount of energy in guarding them. Giving to others is not something that we can do unless we have made a truly awesome resolution. It may be that we could not give our fortune to others or perform service efforts without the steeliest of determination. How difficult would it be for us to perform charitable service for others forever with all the material things we have worked so hard to attain (that is, the "seven treasures")? And how worthy would it be? It is worth giving deeper consideration to why the Buddha spoke so dismissively about charitable service with material things.

Material things, as well as things with form such as honors, privileges, love, beauty, kindness, and knowledge, are not, in the end, eternal. How much time we must invest in accumulating them! Can we realistically possess such a great fortune? How much suffering did we experience in the time it took to accumulate this fortune? Furthermore, when we perform services for others, we will most likely be praised by others. As a result, we will become someone who enjoys privileged treatment wherever he goes, with the result that our mind becomes arrogant and minds of contempt for others emerge within us. Imagine how great the suffering would be if someone were to fail to acknowledge being benefited by our services. Honors, knowledge, privileges—these, too, are relative, and so we are compelled to constantly compare ourselves with others. And when we do, we are constantly seized by torment.

The Buddha tells us that the central presence behind the movement of material things and human minds is the unseen, ungrasped truth that operates the universe. He says that when we engage in definite mind-practice toward awakening to it and instilling it in our mind, the life in which we take the principal value to be locating the truth in the mind, believing in it, and practicing it, is many tens of thousands times more worthy than the life in which we take the principal value to consist only of material and external things such as honors, knowledge, and kindness. For we will be able to enjoy whatever material things are present, without experiencing torment should they be lacking.

This is because we gain the ability to enjoy all material and external honors, privileges, truth, goodness, and beauty when we tame the truth and make it our own.

Only by focusing primarily on the values of the truth in our life and regarding material values as incidental can we live well forever and enjoy a harmonious existence.

Who is the ultimate operator behind this boundless heaven, earth, and nature, the cause of the changes in human society as it passes through rising and falling, prosperity and decline? It is none other than the truth. This is also called by the names of "God" and "the Way." This Dharmakāya is not visible, but it makes all objects obey it and brings about transformations in them. When we substitute this Dharmakāya truth in our mind, traveling with and possessing the truth, we are able to possess all things in this world at will.

Torments and pleasure are produced

entirely according to the seeking mind.

If we can simply adjust the seeking mind,

we will be forever beaming.

When we let go of the searching mind,

we will encounter the ultimate bliss.

Who said the buddhadharma is difficult?

It will be very, very easy.

INTERPRETATION

"How are we to edify the people?"

"Guide them so that they are free from obstruction by the four misleading concepts, the dharma notion, and the non-dharma notion, and thus neither disturbed, nor wrong-doing, nor deluded at any time or place.

"For all worlds of reality are like dreams and illusions, like bubbles and shadows, and when one abides there with one's mind, it will be an illusory life, like morning dew and lightning. You must teach them earnestly and guide them to awaken to this fact."

What Should We Teach Sentient Beings?

The Buddha has presented the core of his teachings. When we edify people, we must first understand what the other person is wishing for, and then share a dharma instruction suited to it. But how are we to ultimately change human lives? We must teach the other to engage in mind-practice. Our minds have all manner of functions. Minds emerge in us that seek to seize when we see privileges, seek to possess when we see money, and seek to love when we see something beautiful. When we see something ugly, a mind of loathing emerges. Such minds are constantly arising, abiding, changing, and disappearing.

These minds are not at all true or eternal. How unfortunate and tormented we will be if we believe these changing minds to represent the truth. We are told that we must teach people to abandon these ever-changing minds—in other words, minds that seek to possess false images. Enemies arise from nearby. When a loving mind collapses greatly, the person becomes a great enemy, and rancor forms within us. Love leads us to the expectation that we must love one another. If, one day, we discover that this is not the case, resentment arises in proportion to our love. Nearly all ordinary people experience torment or pleasure according to the various fixed ideas and preconceptions in their mind. They spend their lives being taken in by these ideas and preconceptions, acting according to their command. This is the life of the traveler in a dream.

The Buddha tells us that we must clear away this life spent living according to fixed ideas, and change course toward a life in which the unchanging true mind is adopted as our master at all times. In all human beings, there exists an unchanging original mind. This is called the "great self," and it may be said to represent the absolute self that we share with the universe. If we can find and recover this unchanging true mind, ours will be the happiest of lives, and when we share the absolute self that is the "universe self," we will abide in the most worthy, ultimate good. This may be called "ultimate bliss" or "paradise." Only when we walk in the great self and original mind realm at all times, appropriately using discriminating minds of charity, love, and faith that are of realistic value, will we have truly tamed the mind well. The important thing, however, is that the most urgent and basic order of business is finding and recovering the original mind.

All Buddhists and clerics engaged in edification can only avoid being captured by fixed ideas when they locate that just-as-it-is mind for themselves. If they do so, there will arise in them true mercy and wisdom like those of the buddha, with the ability to command worthy minds. And teaching everyone with whom we share affinities about the method of using the mind represents the core of what the buddha sought to teach.

What is the reason for Buddhism's existence in this world? It is to build a radiant world through teaching the buddhadharma to the sentient beings of the Saha world. The person who understands this *Diamond Sutra*, and yet neglects to engage in edification through spreading this dharma to others, has either been mistaken in his study of the Sutra or is someone who has not yet achieved maturity. Putting it into practice and teaching it to others as soon as you have understood it is the way for you to repay your debt of gratitude to the Buddha, and to become an agent for the Buddha.

INTERPRETATION

After the Buddha finished speaking, the Venerable Subhuti, the monks and nuns, the male and female lay followers, and all the heavenly beings and asuras rejoiced, respectfully hearing the words of the *Diamond Sutra* instruction and vowing to put them into practice.

To Shine Your Light, You Must Practice Now

The Buddha's dharma power, power of influence, conviction, mercy, and power of persuasion must have wrought tremendous changes in the minds of the audience that listened to *The Diamond Sutra*. How momentous this teaching is for sentient beings who spend their lives pursuing material things, center their lives around good works, or seek merely to satisfy desires! He who receives this great teaching has obtained a truly great light in his eternal life. It may be that those who heard *The Diamond Sutra* when it was first spoken will never forget the grace of the Buddha throughout their eternal lives. Those who were graced with this sacred teaching must have experienced a revolution of the mind within their lives.

For there would have arisen a transformation of the self from worldly values to sacred values. They would have put the dharma instructions into practice in their own lives. And they would have dedicated the utmost zeal to the task of edification by sharing the dharma instruction with others.

We live in this universe.

We meet the central character in heaven and earth

and exchange our respects.

His name is *prajñā* and the one unity image tathāgata;

His age is infinite and unbounded;

His dwelling is within the myriad phenomena of the universe;

His aspect is such that one who claims to have seen

all its facets is mistaken;

His work is such that there is nothing in this universe

that he does not do.

Where are we to look for this master?

If we seek outside, he drifts as far away as we have sought;

But if we turn the *prajñā* wisdom light around and shine it inside,

The hero of the diamond has assumed a place in the central hall.

Do you understand now? Who is reading this right now?

Have you seen it? The one who sees has no eyes.